Transformational Leadership in Nursing

Transformational Leadership in Nursing

Ann Marriner-Tomey, RN, PhD, FAAN

Dean and Professor
Indiana State University
School of Nursing
and
Nursing Management Consultant
Terre Haute, Indiana

Illustrated

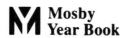 **Mosby**
Year Book

St. Louis   Baltimore   Boston   Chicago   London   Philadelphia   Sydney   Toronto

Mosby
Year Book
Dedicated to Publishing Excellence

Executive Editor: N. Darlene Como
Project Manager: Mark Spann
Production Editors: Daniel J. Johnson, Diane Hoffman
Book Designer: Susan Lane

Printed in the United States of America

Mosby–Year Book, Inc.
11830 Westline Industrial Drive
St. Louis, Missouri 63146

Library of Congress Cataloging-in-Publication Data

Transformational leadership in nursing / [edited by] Ann Marriner-Tomey.
    p.   cm.
    Includes index.
    ISBN 0-8016-6875-1
    1. Nursing services – Administration. 2. Leadership. I. Marriner
-Tomey, Ann, 1943–
    [DNLM: 1. Leadership – nurses' instruction. 2. Nurse
Administrators. 3. Nursing, Supervisory.   WY 105 T772]
RT89.T73 1993
362.1′73068 – dc20
DNLM/DLC   92-15283
for Library of Congress   CIP

93 94 95 96 97   GW/GW/DC   9 8 7 6 5 4 3 2 1

Contributors

JUDITH W. ALEXANDER, RN, PhD
Associate Professor
College of Nursing
University of South Carolina
Columbia, South Carolina

FATIMAH H. AL-KANDARI, RN, DNS
Director of Nursing Program
College of Health Sciences
State of Kuwait
Faiha, Kuwait

DIANA LUSKIN BIORDI, RN, PhD
Associate Professor
College of Nursing
Department of Administrative Studies in Nursing
The University of Illinois at Chicago
Chicago, Illinois

MARY JO BOEGLIN, RN, MSN
Director of Gerontology and Health Services Administration
University of Evansville
Evansville, Indiana

NANCY L. DILLARD, RN, DNS
Assistant Professor, Associate Director
Baccalaureate Nursing Program
School of Nursing
Ball State University
Muncie, Indiana

KAY JACKSON-FRANKL, RN, DNS
Director of Nursing Quality Improvement
Franciscan Health System
Cincinnati, Ohio

JUDITH A HALSTEAD, RN, DNS
Assistant Professor
School of Nursing
Indiana University
Indianapolis, Indiana

ELLEN LYNCH, RN, MSN, EdD
Lecturer
School of Nursing
Indiana University
Indianapolis, Indiana

JUDE A. MAGERS, RN, MSN
Director of Nursing/Clinical Services
St. Vincent Stress Center
Indianapolis, Indiana

ANNA M. MANLEY MCDANIEL, RN, DNS
Assistant Professor
School of Nursing
Ball State University
Muncie, Indiana

VIRGINIA RICHARDSON, RN, CPNP
Assistant Professor
School of Nursing
Indiana University
Indianapolis, Indiana

MARILYN PIEPER SIMONS, RN, MNSN
Assistant Professor
Indiana Wesleyan University
Marion, Indiana

To
LEADERS
and
FOLLOWERS

Preface

The purpose of this book is to describe and advocate the philosophy of transformational leadership, to discuss related concepts and research, and to identify strategies and tools for implementation. It is intended to be an inspirational yet practical resource for nursing leaders. In this rapidly changing environment, we need leaders, not just managers. Warren Bennis has stated that managers do things right while leaders do the right things. Tranformational leaders help give an organization vision and help translate that vision into reality.[1]

The primary audience is students and practitioners of nursing administration, but it can be used as a discussion of leadership for any situation. The content is applied to numerous practice settings through the use of case studies at the end of each chapter. Each chapter begins with chapter objectives, discusses concepts and related research, and discusses implications for nursing. Each case study is followed by questions for discussion.

The book is organized around the strategies Warren Bennis and Burt Nanus identified in their research about leaders: attention through vision, meaning through communication, trust through positioning, deployment of self, and empowerment.

Chapter 1 outlines the history of leadership thought, identifies differences between managers and leaders, and discusses the social, technological, and health care trends that make leadership more important than ever before. Chapter 2 compares charisma, transactional, and transformational leadership. Charisma is the leader's ability to communicate a vision with which followers want to identify. Charismatic leadership makes organizational change effective in response to challenges in the environment. The transformational leader

---

[1]Bennis, W. and Nanus, B.: *Leaders: the strategies for taking charge,* New York, 1985, Harper & Row.

xi

motivates others to perform beyond expectations by empowering them with a sense of commitment to a mission.

Chapter 3 addresses the strategy of meaning through communication. The discussion of leadership as management of meaning includes an overview to the meaning of meaning and management as a symbolic action. The role of language and metaphors as symbols of organizational culture and activity is explored, particularly as it relates to managing change and ambiguity.

Trust can be established through ethical leadership. Chapter 4 examines traditional ethical models and shows the direction of change that will accommodate the different demands of groups of health care workers who espouse a work ideology and associated ethical system. These systems range from the extremely secular to the extremely sacred. The changing demographics of the population in the United States are shaping the future of the health care workers of tomorrow. Health work, in which 75% of the workers are female, is, nevertheless, controlled by men. However, future workers will increasingly be drawn from previously overlooked populations: racial minorities, new immigrants, mature individuals, and even more women. Too many baby boomers with high expectations will likely strive for even fewer management positions, with the potential of glut at the top, high management turnover, redefinitions of success, and older individuals holding tightly to their controlling positions in administration and the workforce. As the new workers, the traditional workforce, and administrators, operate in the health care system, with its current proliferation of models of care delivery, the prevailing ethical system in health care will be challenged.

Chapter 5 discusses the concept of culture and its relevance to leadership. Identifying and closing culture gaps are addressed. A model emphasizing the need for leadership to develop a health care culture supporting assumptions and values necessary in the twenty first century is presented.

Deployment of self is accomplished through shared governance, which is discussed in chapter 6. Chapter 7 discusses theories that deal with the personality characteristics emphasizing the Myers-Briggs types indicator and the importance of knowing and using individual differences.

Chapter 8 discusses organizational socialization as a process by which selected values, behaviors, and social knowledge are communicated to individuals, thus enhancing the individual's ability to function within the organization. The leader's role in providing effective socialization experiences is examined within the framework of the Social Learning Theory. Modeling of desired organizational values and behaviors by the leader is described as one method by which organizational socialization can take place. Chapter 9 describes the value of hardiness in relation to organization culture. The development of hardiness in followers is discussed as the leader models commitment, control, and challenge behaviors.

Technology is a means to empowerment. Chapter 10 explores the technology of health care organizations, using such concepts as task predictability, analyzability, instability, variability, and uncertainty. Emphasis is placed on technology as an environmental condition that is uncertain and dynamic. The analysis will be conducted with the purpose of drawing specific implications for leadership based on the existing technology.

Chapter 11 discusses how leadership styles, traits, abilities, and behaviors influence decision making. Several decision-making models are presented. Strategies for stimulating creativity and innovation are discussed.

Finally, chapter 12 examines the viability of health care organizations within the uncertain and rapidly changing health care system. The importance of intra- and interorganizational networking is explored for its value as a political strategy to enhance power and influence. Organizational networking is used to obtain scarce resources and stimulate diversification so as to extend and expand organizational life and enhance stability. The focus is upon change from a traditional hierarchical structure to one that promotes an entrepreneurial spirit through transformational leadership that uses a positive political strategy. The reciprocal relationship between power and politics is examined. Emphasis is on promoting a positive political strategy that leads to empowerment of individuals and units within an organization that unlocks creativity, enhances innovation, promotes commitment to and ownership in success and the very life of the organization.

Ann Marriner-Tomey

Contents

Trust Through Positioning

Deployment of Self

Empowerment

Transformational Leadership in Nursing

I

Attention Through Vision

1

MARILYN PIEPER SIMONS

Changing Visions
The History of Leadership

CHAPTER OBJECTIVES

- ☐ Discuss the importance to nursing of effective leadership behavior.
- ☐ Describe the development of the meaning, or definition of leadership.
- ☐ Identify the differences between leadership and management.
- ☐ List at least six leadership theories.
- ☐ Explain the evolution of leadership research.

K nowledge and practice of effective leadership behavior are now more essential to nursing than ever before. Nurses must be effective leaders to meet today's challenges. Economics, mergers, downsizing, nursing shortages, nursing salaries, productivity, quality of care, the need to act quickly, and an information glut requiring constant study if one is to remain current are a few of these challenges. Nurses need to be leaders who exercise transformational leadership. Transformational leadership changes followers' visions by using Bennis and Nanus's (1985) suggestions of attention through vision, meaning through communication, trust through positioning, deployment of self, and empowerment. Nursing leaders must realize that people cannot be managed but must be led.

The subject of leadership fascinates people in all walks of life; everyone is affected by leaders. We are affected by our world leaders, by the leaders in our places of employment, and by the leaders in our homes. We study leadership because leaders are essential to achieving the goals of the organization. The organization can be formal, such as in small businesses, large corporations, colleges and universities, or a branch of the armed services. Or the organization can be informal, such as a church group, a neighborhood sports team, a civic association, or a family unit (Stoner and Wankel, 1986).

The scientific study of leadership began in the twentieth century. Early works focused on broad conceptualizations of leadership, such as the behaviors of a leader, and were more comprehensive than their recent counterparts. Current research focuses upon leadership as a process of influencing others within an organizational culture.

Definitions of Leadership

The term *leader* has been in use since the 1300s (*Oxford English Dictionary*, 1933kk). However, the word *leadership* was not known in the English language until the first half of the nineteenth century. Even though it is a relatively new addition to the English language, the term *leadership* has many different meanings. Definitions of leadership are often confusing and unclear because of the use of imprecise terms to describe phenomena such as authority, power, management, administration, control, and supervision (Yukl, 1989). Stogdill (1974, p. 7) states, "There are almost as many definitions of leadership as there are persons who have attempted to define the concept." Yet there is no single definition broad enough to encompass the total leadership process. "Always, it seems, the concept of leadership eludes us or turns up in another form to taunt us again with its slipperiness and complexity. So we have invented an endless proliferation of terms to deal with it . . . and still the concept is not sufficiently defined" (Bennis, 1959, p. 260).

In an effort to decrease this confusion and to conduct empirical tests, researchers often define leadership in their own terms. Leadership has been defined in terms of a focus for group process, personality and its effects, the art of inducing compliance, the exercise of influence, a behavior or act, a form of persuasion, a power relation, an instrument of goal achievement, an emerging effect of interaction, a differentiated role, and the initiation of structure (Bass, 1981).

The definitions of leadership in this chapter start with studies from the early twentieth century and continue to the present. Definitions are categorized by topic areas rather than ordered chronologically because themes are repeated and sometimes span several decades. For instance, the topic of the leader as a focus of group change, activity, and process has examples from 1924, 1957, and 1988. In 1924, Chapin claimed that leadership is a point of polarization for group cooperation. Hemphill and Coons (1957, p. 7) continued with this idea when they stated that leadership is "the behavior of an individual when he is directing the activities of a group toward a shared goal." Kotter (1988, p. 5) established leadership as "the process of moving a group (or groups) in some direction through mostly noncoercive means."

Several early theorists used the concept of personality to explain why some people are better able to exercise leadership than others. Bowden (1926, p. 151) asserted that "indeed the amount of personality attributed to an individual may not be unfairly estimated by the degree of influence he can exert upon others."

The compliance induction theorists regarded leadership as a unidirectional effort of influence and as an instrument to mold the group to the leader's will. Bennis (1959, p. 295) defined leadership as "the process by which an agent induces a subordinate to behave in a desired manner."

The use of the concept "influence" signaled a step in the direction of abstraction and generality in defining leadership. Katz and Kahn (1978, p. 528) provide an example of this in declaring that leadership is "the influential increment over and above mechanical compliance with the routine directives of the organization." In addition, Tannenbaum, Weschler, and Massarik (1961, p. 24) designated leadership as "interpersonal influence, exercised in a situation, and directed, through the communication process, toward the attainment of a specified goal or goals." More recently, Roach and Behling (1984, p. 46) stated that leadership is "the process of influencing the activities of an organized group toward goal achievement."

One group of theorists prefers to use acts or behaviors to define leadership. Fiedler (1967, p. 36) described leadership in such a way when he stated, "By leadership behavior we generally mean the particular acts in which a leader engages in the course of directing and coordinating the work of his group members. This may involve such acts as structuring the work relations, praising or criticizing group members, and showing consideration for their welfare and feelings."

A few early theorists described leadership as persuasion without coercion, while maintaining the leader's role as a determinant in interactions with followers. Schenk (1928) regarded leadership as "the management of men by persuasion and inspiration rather than by the direct or implied threat of coercion." More recently, Bass and Barrett (1981) viewed persuasion as a form of leadership.

By the 1950s, theorists were beginning to describe leadership in terms of power relations. Janda (1960, p. 358) defined leadership as "a particular type of power relationship characterized by a group member's perception that another group member has the right to prescribe behavior patterns for the former regarding his activity as a member of a particular group."

Leadership has been described as an emerging effect of interaction. Merton (1969) perceived leadership as an interpersonal relation in which others comply because they want to, not because they are obligated to.

H.H. Jennings (1944, p. 431) was the first to introduce the idea of leadership as an aspect of role differentiation. He concluded that "leadership thus appears as a manner of interaction involving behavior by and toward the individual 'lifted' to a leader role by other individuals."

Several researchers saw leadership as a process of originating and maintaining role structure rather than acquisition of a role or the passive occupancy of a position. For example, Stogdill (1974, p. 411) suggested that leadership is "the initiation and maintenance of structure in expectation and interaction."

House (1988, p. 253) has described leadership in terms of a process with several variables involved. "Leadership is a social activity involving informal or formal status differences between the leader and the follower, usually face-to-face communication, exertion of social as well as informational influence, usually but not always involving relationships between a leader and a group of subordinates or between a leader and a number of individuals in multiple dyads."

Although there are many differences, the commonality in definitions has to do with a group, a phenomenon where there is an interaction between two or more people (Janda, 1960). Leadership occurs when one person in a group stands out and leads other persons who are then referred to as followers or subordinates (Yukl, 1989). In addition, there is some intentional influence of the leader over the followers.

The controversy over the definition of leadership is not likely to be resolved in the near future. Most researchers empirically define leadership in a manner appropriate for their investigations. Therefore it is necessary to be familiar with a variety of perspectives from theorists and researchers and to accept leadership as a complex and multifaceted phenomenon. Just as the definition of leadership is as yet unclear, controversy also continues over the differences between leadership and management.

Leadership vs. Management

Although some believe that management and leadership are synonymous, Hersey and Blanchard (1982) believe there is an essential distinction between the two concepts. They define leadership as "the process of influencing the activities of an individual or a group in efforts toward goal achievement in a given situation" (p. 83). Management is described as "working with and through individuals and groups to accomplish organizational goals" (p. 3). A common thread found in all definitions is that the manager's interest is in accomplishing organizational objectives and goals. Leadership is a broader concept than management, whereas management is a particular type of leadership in which achievement of organizational goals is essential. The word *organization* is the key difference between the two concepts. Leadership can occur any time the behavior of followers is influenced, whether it is for the leader's goals or those of others. These goals may or may not be a part of organizational goals.

Bennis and Nanus (1985) agree that, although both leadership and management are important, there is a profound difference between the two. They believe that "managers are people who do things right and leaders are people who do the right thing" (p. 21). A manager is one who brings things about, one who accomplishes, one who has responsibility, one who conducts. A leader is one who influences and guides direction, opinion, and courses of action. The difference between leadership and management may be summarized as effectiveness vs. efficiency; whereas effectiveness has to do with activities of vision and judgment, and efficiency is related to activities of mastering routines. Leaders create rather than simply master basic routines. Leadership is the essential force behind successful organizations. Leadership is needed to assist organizations to develop visions of what they can be and then mobilize the forces to change toward the new vision. Today's situation mandates leaders who commit people to action, convert followers into leaders, and transform leaders into change agents (Bennis and Nanus, 1985).

Kotter (1988) asserts that leadership and management are not mutually exclusive; they are complementary and sometimes overlap. Each is needed to

keep the other in check. Without leadership, management can become overbear-
ingly bureaucratic and less creative over time. Without management, leadership
can become overwhelmingly volatile, as exemplified by the madness of Jim Jones
(a preacher who led a mass suicide in South America) and Adolf Hitler.

Yukl (1989) concludes there is general agreement that leadership and
management are different but states that the degree of overlap is where the
controversy lies. A person can be a manager without leading or be a leader
without managing. Often a manager may not have followers (e.g., a manager of
financial accounts). The main difference between leadership and management is
that leaders influence commitment, whereas managers take care of position
responsibilities and exercise authority.

Research Evolution

More can be learned and understood about leadership through developing
theories from which research questions can be derived. Many theorists and
investigators have focused their study upon the concept of leadership. Nearly
10,000 books and articles have been published on the topic of leadership (Yukl,
1989). Scientific research studies of leadership did not begin until around the
beginning of the twentieth century. Since then, several schools of thought
regarding leadership study have prevailed. Early theorists described leadership in
terms of either the individual or the environment and did not consider the nature
of the relationship between the two. They were more comprehensive in theory
development than their more recent counterparts. Behavioral scientists explored
what behaviors, abilities, traits, sources of power, and/or aspects of the situation
determine the leader's ability to influence others and to accomplish group
objectives. In recent decades, investigators have viewed leadership as part of role
differentiation or as derived from social interaction processes (Bass, 1981).

Leadership researchers have concentrated their investigations on various
areas of the population, such as students, military personnel, and business
managers, and they have essentially ignored other segments, such as politicians,
labor leaders, and criminals. Recently, new areas of leadership have been explored
(e.g., nurses, case workers, police, and minorities, including women and blacks).
In addition, the number of cross-cultural leadership studies has recently increased
(Bass, 1981).

Although much valuable information has been obtained, there is still much
that is not understood regarding leadership. The knowledge base has not grown
much over time. In 1959, Bennis (pp. 259, 260) wrote that "probably more has
been written and less known about leadership than any other topic in the
behavioral sciences." Stogdill (1974, p. vii) concluded, "It is difficult to know
what, if anything, has been convincingly demonstrated by replicated research.

The endless accumulation of empirical data has not produced an integrated understanding of leadership." By 1978, Burns (p. 2) admitted that "leadership is one of the most observed and least understood phenomena on earth." More recently, Yukl (1989) asserted that with the various controversies about conceptual and methodological issues, the field of leadership is in a state of flux. Reviewing the research shows that we know more about leadership than we thought but not as much as we need to know. Although the predominant question that has been investigated pertains to leadership effectiveness, there is a need to develop and research other important questions about why some people emerge as leaders and about the determinants for the manner in which the leader acts (Yukl, 1989).

The nagging question continues: "What makes an effective leader?" So far, researchers have not identified a quick recipe for an effective leader, one who has instant success. In part, the lack of knowledge regarding leadership stems from the controversy concerning whether quantitative or qualitative research methodology is appropriate. Another major portion of the knowledge deficit results from vagueness in the definition of leadership, making empirical studies difficult.

As indicated in an earlier discussion, the topic of leadership has been studied in different ways. Investigators have different methodological preferences and their own concepts of leadership. Researchers tend to focus more and more on a narrow aspect of leadership for study. The major theories of leadership from which research questions are derived are outlined in the next section.

Leadership Theories

Leadership theories reveal the nature and history of leadership thought. Empirical research is closely related to theory development. Derived questions test theories, and then the theories are either validated or modified appropriately. Most leadership theories can be classified under these approaches: great man theory, trait theory, charismatic theory, situational theories, contingency theory, path-goal theory, life-cycle theory, and transformational leadership theory.

Great Man Theory

What makes a leader? What makes a leader great? The "great man" theory is based on the premise that select people are born with the necessary characteristics to be great. Great man theorists attempted to explain leadership on the basis of inheritance. Examples of the great man theorists are Woods (1913) and Wiggam (1931). Great man leaders are well-rounded and possess both supportive and instrumental leadership behaviors. Instrumental activities to accomplish the organization's goals include planning, organizing, and controlling activities of followers. Especially important is obtaining and allocating resources such as people, equipment, funds, space, and materials. Supportive leadership has a social orientation and permits participation and consultation from followers for decisions that affect them. "Great men" are people who use both instrumental and supportive leadership behaviors and are effective leaders in any situation (Marriner-Tomey, 1992). Opponents of this theory protest that leadership can be developed and that the necessary characteristics are not just inherited (Fiedler and Chemers, 1974).

Trait Theory

Trait theory was the basis for most leadership research until the mid-1940s. Trait theory research is closely related to the great man theory. Early theorists believed that if leaders inherit superior qualities that make them stand out from their followers, then these traits could be singled out and studied. Most leadership theorists attributed leader success to superior abilities, such as irresistable persuasive powers, tireless energy, uncanny foresight, and penetrating intuition (Yukl, 1989).

L. L. Bernard (1926), Bingham (1927), Tead (1929), and Kilbourne (1935) described leadership in relation to traits of personality and character. Smith and Krueger (1933) completed an investigation of leadership traits for educators, and Jenkins (1947) described military leadership. Bird (1940) used 20 psychologically oriented studies to complete a list of leadership traits, including such values as the following:

Adaptable	Entertaining	Kind	Self-composed
Aggressive	Enthusiastic	Loyal	Self-confident
Ambitious	Extroverted	Mature	Self-reliant
Amusing	Fair	Mild	Sincere
Brave	Fluent	Neat	Sociable
Brilliant	Frank	Noble	Stable
Clever	Friendly	Open-minded	Sympathetic
Competent	Healthy	Organized	Tactful
Cooperative	Humorous	Original	Talkative
Decisive	Imaginative	Persistent	Versatile
Devoted	Industrious	Poised	Well-informed
Dignified	Insightful	Purposeful	
Diplomatic	Just	Reliable	

Although trait theory has added to knowledge of leadership, it is not without its flaws. Few traits are identified in all trait theory research. There is considerable overlap among definitions, and the traits are not mutually exclusive. It is not clear which traits are essential to acquire and/or maintain leadership. In addition, trait theory does not perceive personality as an integrated whole, does not deal with followers, and omits environmental and situational factors (Marriner-Tomey, 1992).

Charismatic Theory

The quality of charisma holds a fascination for many theorists. Despite numerous research projects, little is known regarding this intangible subject. The charismatic leader is usually confident and dominant, has a sense of purpose, and possesses the ability to articulate the objectives and ideas for which the followers have already been psychologically prepared (House, 1977). The charismatic leader arouses strong feelings of loyalty and enthusiasm by inspiring and obtaining emotional commitment from followers (Marriner-Tomey, 1992). The charismatic leader accomplishes the seemingly impossible.

Weber (1947) first used the term to describe a form of influence based upon the followers' belief that the leader is endowed with special qualities. House (1977) developed a theory of charismatic leadership based on findings from diverse social science disciplines. His theory describes how such leaders behave, distinctive characteristics they possess, and situations in which the charismatic leader is most likely to thrive. Bass (1985) extended House's theory (1977) to include leadership attributes, additional antecedent conditions, and consequences of charismatic leadership. More recently, Conger and Kanungo (1987) have described a theory based on the premise that charismatic leadership is an attributional phenomenon.

Situational Theory

During the late 1940s and early 1950s, situational theories became popular. Situation theories propose that traits required for leadership vary with the situation. Because the kind of leadership needed depends upon the situation, a person may be a leader in one situation and a follower in another (Marriner-Tomey, 1992).

Stogdill (1948) suggested that traits required for leadership must have some relationship to characteristics of the followers; an adequate investigation of leadership also includes a study of the situation. Stogdill's work (1948) set the stage for future situational theorists. Gerth and Mills (1952) concluded that four items must be examined to understand leadership: (1) traits and motives of the individual leader, (2) public image of the leader and motive for the public to follow the leader, (3) features of the leadership role, and (4) the particular situation in which the leader and followers are involved.

Contingency Theory

In his contingency model, Fiedler (1967) proposed that the effectiveness of a given pattern of leader behavior is dependent upon the interaction of the personality of the leader and the challenges dictated by the situation. Task-oriented leaders are most likely to be effective in situations that are most favorable or most unfavorable to them as leaders. The situations between the two extremes are where the relations-oriented leader is most apt to be effective. If a leader is esteemed by his or her followers, if the specified task is simple, clear, structured, and easy to solve, and if the leader has power and legitimacy, then a situation is favorable to the leader. Fiedler emphasized the need to place leaders in the situations for which they are best suited. More recently, Fiedler, Chemers, and Mahar (1976) have proposed "leader match" training, in which the leader of designated orientation (task-oriented or relations-oriented) is assisted to adapt to the situation.

Path-Goal Theory

House (1971) popularized the path-goal theory of leadership, which proffers that leaders motivate followers to perform by achieving satisfaction from the task to be accomplished. Leaders clarify goals and the paths to those goals with their followers. The leader enhances task accomplishment by minimizing obstructions to goals and offering followers rewards for completing their tasks (Marriner-Tomey, 1992). House and Mitchell (1974) warn that because they see the relatively new path-goal theory as having the potential for adding new knowledge to describe leadership, this theory should be used more as a tool to direct research than as a proven guide for managerial action.

Life-Cycle Theory/Situational Leadership

Hersey and Blanchard (1982) developed the life-cycle theory of leadership, which is now known as situational leadership. This theory synthesizes Blake and Mouton's (1964) managerial grid propositions, Reddin's (1977) 3-D effectiveness typology, and Argyris's (1964) maturity-immaturity theory. In Hersey and Blanchard's (1982) theory, the maturity of followers relates to leader behavior; as the maturity of followers increases, leader behavior should reflect a decreased emphasis on task structure and a greater emphasis on consideration. There should be an eventual decrease in consideration as maturity increases and the person consequently needs less support. Maturity is described with respect to the followers' experience, achievement, motivation, and ability and willingness to accept responsibility (Hersey and Blanchard, 1982).

Transformational Leadership

There is considerable overlap between charismatic and transformational leadership; however, transformational leadership is usually described in broader terms than charismatic leadership. Burns (1978, p. 20) has defined transformational leadership as a process in which "leaders and followers raise one another to higher levels of motivation and morality." Transformational leaders strive to elevate the consciousness of followers by appealing to higher ideals and moral values such as humanitarianism, liberty, equality, justice, and peace. Emotions such as fear, jealousy, greed, and hatred are subdued. Bennis and Nanus (1985, p. 3) refer to a transformational leader as a "new leader," a leader who "commits people to action, who converts followers into leaders, and who converts leaders into agents of change." Through their research, they have identified four leadership strategies: attention through vision, meaning through communication, trust through positioning, and deployment of self. Empowerment is considered a dependent variable.

◻ Implications for Nursing

Researchers attempt to increase the understanding of leadership when they define the concept in terms of the focus of their investigations. The research focus has gone from a broad scope to a more narrow focus and from the individual to the process. Some valuable information has been obtained to assist in understanding leadership; however, research regarding leadership should continue so that knowledge can be provided to fill in the gaps, settle controversy, and define effective leadership, whether it is in the context of formal or informal organizations.

Leadership practices in nursing should be based upon empirical processes that can serve as guides for practice and behavior. Transformational leadership, as suggested by Bennis and Nanus (1985), is an example of a process that could be a guide for nursing. Little theoretical or research work can be found in the nursing literature specific to transformational leadership. Nursing needs to identify transformational leadership behaviors and practices so they can be rewarded and modeled by others.

◻ Application to Nursing: Case Study

Carol Palmer is the patient care coordinator of a 12-bed coronary care step-down unit. Carol started on the unit as a graduate nurse 5 years ago and has been the coordinator for the past 2 years. She is currently working on a Master of Nursing Administration degree. She has established good rapport with her colleagues and staff and is popular with the patients and their family members. Carol is an excellent clinician who is highly skilled and proficient. She is a wise and respected administrator, possibly because of her professionalism and insight. She is perceived by her followers as being direct, flexible, understanding, positive, and supportive. Two new graduate nurses have just started their orientation on her unit. As part of the orientation program, Carol gave them a list of procedures they needed to complete within two weeks. The orientees notice that Carol is extremely professional with them in orienting them to procedures and expectations, but not as friendly as she is with her other staff members.

Discussion Questions

1. What leadership characteristics does Carol exhibit? Are these characteristics effective?
2. How does Hersey and Blanchard's (1982) theory apply to this situation?
3. Using Hersey and Blanchard's (1982) definition, describe the maturity level of the orientees.
4. Was the level of task structure and consideration appropriate for this situation?
5. Are there other leadership theories that apply in this situation?

References

Argyris, C. (1964). *Integrating the individual and the organization.* New York: Wiley.

Bass, B.M. (1981). *Stogdill's handbook of leadership: A survey of theory and research.* New York: The Free Press.

Bass, B.M. (1985). *Leadership and performance beyond expectations.* New York: The Free Press.

Bass, B.M. & Barrett, G.V. (1981). *People, work and organizations: An introduction to industrial and organizational psychology.* Boston: Allyn & Bacon.

Bennis, W. (1959). Leadership theory and administrative behavior: The problems of authority. *Administration Science Quarterly, 4,* 259-301.

Bennis, W. & Nanus, B. (1985). *Leaders: The strategies for taking charge.* New York: Harper & Row.

Bernard, L.L. (1926). *An introduction to social psychology.* New York: Holt.

Bingham, W.V. (1927). Leadership. In J.C. Metcalf, (Ed.) *The psychological foundations of management.* New York: Shaw.

Bird, C. (1940). *Social psychology.* New York: Appleton-Century.

Blake, R.R. & Moulton, J.S. (1964). *The managerial grid.* Houston: Gulf.

Bowden, A.O. (1926). A study of the personality of student leaders in the United States. *Journal of Abnormal Sociological Psychology, 21,* 149-160.

Burns, J.M. (1978). *Leadership.* New York: Harper and Row.

Burns, J.M. (1982). *Leadership.* New York: Harper and Row.

Chapin, F.S. (1924). Socialized leadership. *Social Forces, 3,* 57-60.

Conger, J.A. & Kanungo, R. (1987). Toward a behavioral theory of charismatic leadership in organizational settings. *Academy of Management Review, 12,* 637-647.

Fiedler, F.E. (1967). *A theory of leadership effectiveness.* New York: McGraw-Hill.

Fiedler, F.E. & Chemers, M.M. (1974). *Leadership and effective management.* Glenview, Illinois: Scott Foresman and Co.

Fiedler, F.E., Chemers, M.M., & Mahar, L. (1976). *Improving leadership effectiveness: The leader match concept.* New York: John Wiley & Sons, Inc.

Gerth, H. & Mills, C.W. (1952). A sociological note on leadership. In J.E. Julett & R. Stagner (Eds.), *Problems in social psychology.* Urbana, Ill: University of Illinois Press.

Gibb, J.R. (1954). *Factors producing defensive behavior within groups.* Boulder: University of Colorado, Human Relations Lab., Annual Technical Report.

Hemphill, J.K. & Coons, A.E. (1957). Development of the leader behavior description questionnaire. In R.M. Stogdill and A.E. Coons (Eds.). *Leader behavior: Its description and measurement.* Columbus: Ohio State University, Bureau of Business Research.

Hersey, P. & Blanchard, K.H. (1982). *Management of organizational behavior: Utilizing human resources.* Englewood Cliffs, NJ: Prentice-Hall.

House, R.J. (1971). A path-goal theory of leader effectiveness. *Administration Science Quarterly, 16,* 321-338.

House, R.J. (1977). A 1976 theory of charismatic leadership. In J.G. Hunt & L.L. Larson (Eds.), *Leadership: The cutting edge.* Carbondale: Southern Illinois University Press.

House, R.J. (1988). Leadership research: Some forgotten, ignored, or overlooked findings. In J.G. Hunt, B.R. Baliga, H.P. Dachler, & C.A. Schriesheim (Eds.), *Emerging Leadership Vistas* (pp. 245-260). Lexington: Lexington Books, D.C. Heath & Co.

House, R.J. & Mitchell, T.R. (1974). Path-goal theory of leadership. *Journal of Contemporary Business, 3,* 81-97.

Janda, K.F. (1960). Toward the explication of the concept of leadership in terms of the concept of power. *Human Relations, 13,* 345-363.

Jenkins, W.O. (1947). A review of leadership studies with particular reference to military problems. *Psychological Bulletin, 44,* 54-79.

Jennings, H.H. (1944). Leadership—a dynamic redefinition. *Journal of Educational Sociology, 17,* 431-433.

Katz, D. & Kahn, R.L. (1978). *The social psychology of organizations.* (2nd Ed.) New York: John Wiley.

Kilborne, C.E. (1935). The elements of leadership. *Journal of Coast Artillery, 78,* 437-439.

Kotter, J.P. (1988). *The leadership factor.* New York: The Free Press.

Marriner-Tomey, A. (1992). *Guide to nursing management.* (4th Ed.). St. Louis: Mosby—Year Book, Inc.

Merton, R.K. (1969). The social nature of leadership. *American Journal of Nursing, 69,* 2614-2618.

The Oxford English Dictionary (Volume VII). (1933). Oxford: At the Clarendon Press.

Reddin, W.J. (1977). An integration of leader-behavior typologies. *Group Organizational Studies, 2,* 282-295.

Roach, C.F. & Behling, O. (1984). Functionalism: Basis for an alternate approach to the study of leadership. In J.G. Hunt, D.M. Hosking, C.A. Schriesheim, & R. Steward (Eds.), *Leaders and managers: International perspectives on managerial behavior and leadership.* Elmsford, NY: Pergamon Press.

Schenk, C. (1928). Leadership. *Infantry Journal, 33,* 111-112.

Smith, H.L. & Krueger, L.M. (1933). *A brief summary of literature on leadership.* Bloomington: Indiana University, School of Education Bulletin.

Stogdill, R.M. (1948). Personal factors associated with leadership: A survey of the literature. *Journal of Psychology, 25,* 35-71.

Stogdill, R.M. (1974). *Stogdill's handbook of leadership: A survey of theory and research.* New York: The Free Press.

Stoner, J.A.F. & Wankel, C. (1986). *Management* (3rd ed.). Englewood Cliffs, NJ: Prentice-Hall, Inc.

Tannenbaum, R., Weschler, I.R., & Massarik, R. (1961). *Leadership and organization.* New York: McGraw-Hill.

Tead, O. (1929). The technique of creative leadership. In *human nature and management.* New York: McGraw-Hill.

Weber, M. (1947). *The theory of social and economic organization.* New York: Oxford University Press.

Wiggam, A.E. (1931). The biology of leadership. In H.C. Metcalf (Ed.), *Business leadership.* New York: Pitman.

Woods, F.A. (1913). *The influence of monarchs.* New York: Macmillan.

Yukl, G.A. (1989). *Leadership in organizations* (2nd ed.). Englewood Cliffs, NJ: Prentice Hall.

2

ANNA M. MANLEY MCDANIEL

Beyond Charisma
Transformational Leadership

CHAPTER OBJECTIVES

☐ Compare and contrast charismatic and transformational leadership.

☐ Describe the two forms of leadership according to Burns.

☐ Discuss the three components of transformational leadership as described by Bass.

☐ Explain the relationship between leadership and personality development.

☐ Identify at least three follower characteristics associated with transformational leadership.

☐ Discuss the effect of specific leadership strategies in organizational transformation.

This chapter presents an overview of the major theories and research findings on charismatic and transformational leadership. Transformational leadership in complex modern organizations is a process of influencing organizational members to achieve shared goals. The transformational leader motivates others to perform beyond expectations by empowering followers with a sense of commitment to a mission. Charisma is the leader's ability to communicate a vision with which followers want to identify. Charismatic leadership empowers organizational change in response to challenges in the environment. This chapter discusses charisma as a component of the transformational leadership process. All transformational leaders have charisma, but transformational leadership goes beyond charismatic leadership to transform followers.

Charismatic Leadership

Max Weber (1947) was the first social scientist to describe charisma. His book, *The Theory of Social and Economic Organization,* provides an explanation for the existence of authority in social groups, including work groups. Authority is the right of one individual to exercise control over others in a social system. According to Weber (1947) three types of authority exist, either alone or in combination: (1) rational-legal authority, (2) traditional authority, and (3) charismatic authority.

Rational-legal authority exists in situations in which the right to authority is based on a formal body of rules or laws. Leaders in bureaucratic organizations wield this authority over followers by virtue of their position or office. Rational-legal authority is limited to the specific domain of the bureaucracy. Followers obey the bureaucratic leader within this sphere out of obligation to the organization. No obligation to the leader exists outside of the bureaucratic relationship, and thus the leader exercises no control over followers in other settings.

Traditional authority is the second form of authority that Weber (1947) describes. Leaders who exert traditional authority do so out of status accorded by traditional rules of order rather than laws. These rules have been transmitted from the beliefs of generations past. People obey the traditional leader because of loyalty to the person who occupies a position held in esteem by the group. The traditional leader's power is determined by the limitations imposed by the traditional order. A monarchy is an example of traditional authority.

Charismatic authority contrasts with both rational and traditional authority; charismatic authority conflicts with, rather than exists within, the established social structure. Charismatic authority is a revolutionary force for change in the traditional rules of order or formal laws governing behavior.

Charisma is defined by Weber (1947, p. 358) as "a certain quality of an individual personality by virtue of which he is set apart from ordinary men and treated as endowed with supernatural, superhuman, or at least specifically exceptional powers or qualities." Charismatic authority is bestowed upon the leader by followers who ascribe these qualities to the leader. Obligation to obey the charismatic leader comes not from any formal set of rules but rather from the sense of moral duty felt by the followers.

To be recognized by followers as charismatic, the leader must demonstrate extraordinary abilities and communicate a vision of a new social structure. Followers are inspired by the charismatic leader's mission and believe in the leader's ability to transcend the existing boundaries of authority. Total devotion to leaders and their missions is typical in charismatic groups. This devotion often extends to all areas of the follower's life.

According to Weber's theory (1947), "pure" charisma exists only in the process of originating a new social structure. Because charismatic authority rests within an individual perceived to be above the ordinary, charismatic leadership cannot remain stable. However, charismatic authority may be transformed into a permanent authority structure that Weber calls "routinized" charisma.

Charismatic authority can be routinized in one of two ways. First, charisma may be transferred to another leader through leadership succession. This may occur in a variety of ways such as heredity, designation by the original leader, ritual, or group consensus. The second form of routinization is the transformation of charismatic authority from the person to the office or leadership position. Thus, charismatic authority becomes a form of traditional or rational authority.

Empirical studies of charismatic leadership based on Weber's theory (1947) have been limited. One possible reason for the dearth of research in this area is the abstract nature of concepts such as "superhuman abilities" and "trancendence." Studies that have focused on charisma have primarily examined the characteristics of famous political leaders such as Hitler, Gandhi, and Churchill (Schweitzer, 1984; Trice & Beyer, 1986; Willner, 1984).

Dow (1969) refined the theory of charisma based on an analysis of Weber's original work (1947). According to Dow (1969), charisma is an empirically observable phenomenon. Charisma involves a unique relationship between leader and followers rather than only a personality trait of the leader. A charismatic relationship exists when the leader communicates a plan for revolutionary change to which the followers adhere because of their belief in the extraordinary capabilities of the leader. The charismatic leader has appeal to followers on an emotional level, based on their perceptions of the leader's revolutionary image. This type of relationship is possible at any time in the development of any social or work group.

House (1977) presents a theory of charismatic leadership as a set of potentially testable propositions. Charismatic leadership can be defined in terms of the effects the leader has on followers, including trust, obedience, and emulation. According to House (1977), these effects can be explained by the complex interactions of the charismatic leader's characteristics, his or her behaviors, and the situational factors present in the overall social context.

Three characteristics of charismatic leaders are (1) self-confidence, (2) dominance, and (3) a strong conviction of the moral righteousness of their mission. House (1977) hypothesizes that charismatic leaders also have a high need to influence others. These characteristics are the factors that motivate the leader to develop a charismatic relationship with a group of followers.

A charismatic leader produces charismatic effects on followers by engaging in a set of behaviors. Leaders who model the values and beliefs they desire in followers are likely to inspire loyalty to themselves and their goals. The charismatic leader takes action that alone creates the impression of competence. Another behavior that is characteristic of the charismatic leader is the communication of high expectations of the followers' abilities to achieve a goal. This enhances self-esteem in followers and motivates followers to accomplish the mission.

Situational variables also play a part in the development of a charismatic relationship. House (1977) does not describe the nature of situational factors necessary for charismatic leadership to emerge but states merely that an "opportunity" for goal articulation must be present for a leader to have charismatic effects (p. 204).

Bradley (1987) studied the structural foundation of charisma in communal groups. Bradley (1987) asserts that charisma is more than the personal influence of leaders and that it goes beyond a social relationship between leaders and their followers. According to Bradley (1987), charisma is a distinctive pattern of social organization. A charismatic system involves the interrelationship between communion and power. Communion, the emotional bonds between group members, generates the energy required for social change. This energy is highly unstable and must be balanced by the controlling power of the charismatic leader. Bradley (1987) postulates that the charismatic social organization evolves to meet the needs of group members within the situational context.

Conger and Kanungo (1987) present an integrated framework of charismatic leadership in organizational settings. Charisma is an attribute assigned by followers who observe a constellation of behaviors in a leader. Four variables determine the leader's charisma:

1. The degree of inconsistency between the status quo and the leader's vision
2. The use of unconventional and innovative strategies to achieve goals
3. The accuracy of the leader's assessment of environmental conditions that support or inhibit change
4. The articulation of a mission that inspires followers

Contextual factors play an important role in the development of charismatic leadership in this model. Situations that predispose followers to seek or anticipate change facilitate the emergence of a charismatic leader. The leader who is sensitive to contextual factors creates the perceived need for change in the followers. This is the first step in transforming group members' attitudes into a shared vision.

Although the more current theories of charismatic leadership have postulated testable research hypotheses, few additional scientific investigations have been reported. Charisma as an empirical phenomenon remains difficult to measure. Trice and Beyers (1986) identified the components of charisma in their analysis of two charismatic leaders. Criteria for identification of charisma were developed. These included:

1. Exceptional personal qualities of the leader
2. A perceived social crisis
3. A radical message
4. A set of followers inspired by the leader's vision
5. Validation of the leader's gifts by visible success

Conger (1989) compared charismatic and noncharismatic business executives through interviews, observation, and analysis of company documents. Based on the results of this investigation, Conger (1989) believes that charismatic leadership may exist as a scalar (on a continuum) rather than a dichotomous (either/or) variable. Behavioral attributes of charismatic leaders have been identified as an initial step in the development of instruments to measure the phenomenon of charismatic leadership (Conger & Kanungo, 1988). To explore the antecedents and effects of charismatic leadership, more research to establish the validity of the charismatic leadership model must be completed.

Transformational Leadership

Transformational leadership is a leadership paradigm that has several similarities to charismatic leadership. While charismatic leadership describes the relationship between the leader and followers, transformational leadership provides a broader perspective that takes into account the complexity of organizational culture. Charisma is one component of the overall leadership process. An overview of transformational leadership theories and relevant empirical findings will be presented in this section.

In his book, *Leadership* (1978), Burns states that a leadership crisis exists today because of inadequate knowledge of the leadership process. To Burns, an understanding of the nature of leadership lies in the fundamental differences between leadership and power. Both power and leadership are relationships between leaders and followers, not phenomena unto themselves. Both relationships involve motivation, resources, and influence. Power is exercised when the leader mobilizes resources that influence followers' behavior relevant to the leader's goals. Leadership occurs, on the other hand, when the leader mobilizes resources that satisfy the motives of the followers.

Burns (1978) sees leadership as a special form of power. Motivations of the leader and followers determine which of two forms the leadership will take. Burns (1978) calls these forms of leadership transactional and transforming.

Transactional leadership occurs when a leader initiates a relationship with followers based on exchange. In this relationship the leader motivates the desired follower behavior in exchange for some resource that is valued by the follower. Interaction between leader and followers is limited to the exchange transaction. The effects of transactional leadership are episodic and short-lived.

Burns (1978) contrasts transactional leadership with the more complex process of transforming leadership. "Such leadership occurs when one or more persons engage with others in such a way that leaders and followers raise one another to higher levels of motivation and morality" (Burns, 1978, p. 20). The motives of the leader and followers become identical through the transforming process. This relationship transforms both parties by raising the "level of human conduct and ethical aspiration of both leader and led" (Burns, 1978, p. 20).

The potential for conflict exists in all relationships and may be either a positive or negative force for change. Transforming leaders use conflict to exert influence by making followers aware of their needs and wants. Transforming leadership operates toward a conscious purpose to exploit the tension within followers' value systems. Resolving the conflicts of values among followers elevates the level of moral values toward equality, freedom, and justice.

According to Burns' theory (1978), transforming leadership shapes and alters the goals and values of followers to achieve a collective purpose that benefits society. The true test of leadership is intentional change in the whole, brought about through the leader's decisions and actions. Transforming leadership is the collectively purposeful causation of change within the group (Burns, 1978).

Bass (1985a) extends Burns' theory (1978) of political leadership to complex organizational settings. They both define leadership similarly in terms of effects on followers. However, Burns (1978) proposes that transactional and transforming are two separate forms of leadership, whereas Bass's (1985a) model incorporates elements of both types.

Both authors view transactional leadership as an exchange relationship. The transactional leader recognizes and clarifies the task requirements for followers. This instills confidence and motivates expected performance. The leader, in turn, rewards the followers' efforts in response to their self-interests.

The transformational leader moves followers to transcend their own self-interests for higher goals. Through articulation and role modeling, the transformational leader heightens the followers' awareness of what needs to be done to accomplish the shared goal. This elevates followers to a level of autonomous self-regulation and motivates them to perform beyond their original expectations.

According to Bass (1985a), there are three components of transformational leadership. These factors are highly interrelated and are always present to some degree in transformational leadership. These components are (1) charisma, (2) individualized consideration, and (3) intellectual stimulation.

Charisma is not confined to world class political leaders but is also found in complex organizational settings such as business and industry, education, and the military. The charismatic leader inspires followers to loyalty to a cause. Charismatic leaders are seen by followers as possessing special qualities that evoke strong emotional reactions. Followers want to identify with a charismatic leader.

All transformational leaders are charismatic, but not all charismatic leaders transform followers. Popular celebrities are a case in point. What sets the transformational leader apart from the mere charismatic is the ability to arouse the motivation of followers to accomplish the mission. The transformational leader does this by articulating the importance of the vision and communicating confidence in followers' abilities (Bass, 1985a).

Individualized consideration contributes to follower satisfaction and productivity. Respect for the individuality of each follower is demonstrated by activities such as expressing appreciation, counseling, and encouraging follower performance. Frequent, informal communication is typical of this leadership dimension. The transformational leader who has an individualized orientation often delegates responsibilities and assumes a mentor role with followers. Individualized consideration enhances follower self-esteem and confidence, which then increases performance. Individualized consideration can be divisive, however, if followers perceive the leader's behavior as inequitable.

Leaders who provide intellectual stimulation arouse awareness and activate problem-solving capabilities in followers. Transformational leaders project new ideas through the manipulation of language and symbols, such as slogans and rituals. Transformational leaders are proactive and innovative in thinking; transactional leaders are reactive.

Bass (1985a) identifies two factors present in the exchange relationship of transactional leadership. These factors—contingent reward and management by exception—are closely related. The leader who consistently reinforces the expected follower performance to influence motivation exemplifies contingent reward. In management by exception, the transactional leader intervenes only with negative feedback only when something goes wrong. Negative feedback may be counter-productive if the leader does not diagnose the problem correctly. Preference of one form of transactional leadership over the other may be partially determined by the traditions and expectations of the organizational culture.

Effective leaders may exhibit the characteristics of transactional leadership, transformational leadership, or both, depending on the situation. The situation is determined by the external environment, the organizational dynamics, and the personality and values of the leader. A crisis in the external environment often precipitates the rise of a transformational leader with charisma. Transactional leadership frequently prevails in highly structured, bureaucratic organizations. Environmental and structural variables interact with the distinct personal qualities of the leader either to transform or reinforce the existing organizational culture.

Kuhnert and Lewis (1987) propose a framework for understanding the personality differences between transactional and transformational leaders. This framework is based on Robert Kegan's Constructive/Developmental Theory (1982). According to this theory, humans construct a subjective view of reality that follows increasingly complex patterns. These patterns form the matrix of the personality that generates the individual's thoughts, emotions, and behavior.

Subject and object are two personality structures that shape a person's perceptions of the world. People construct experience through the subject. Subject is the frame of reference (of which the individual is unaware) for organizing all human experiences. The perceived content of these experiences is object. The individual is able to consciously contemplate the object of experience.

Through the developmental process, people alter their ways of construing reality. What is subject at earlier stages of development comes into the person's object awareness at higher levels. Kuhnert and Lewis (1987) propose that the differences between transactional and transformational leaders can be explained by this theoretical perspective.

Transactional leaders organize their world based on personal goals and agendas. All their experiences are cognitively processed in these terms. At this level, leaders are aware of only their personal needs and feelings and assume that followers are also motivated by personal interests. The exchange approach is the logical outcome of this view of the leadership relationship.

As individuals develop, they may progress to the next stage, where they become aware of the interests of others. Leaders at this level of development organize their world based on mutual obligations. Transactional leaders at this stage depend upon mutual respect to motivate behavior, yet interaction remains at the exchange level.

Transformational leaders organize their world on the basis of their personal values. The leader at this stage of development is able to transcend personal agendas and have an objective view of interpersonal commitments. Because transformational leaders operate from their personal value systems, they attempt to motivate followers by integrating these values into the group. These leaders transform followers' beliefs and attitudes.

Though empirical support for constructive/developmental personality theory is limited at this time, Kuhnert and Lewis (1987) provide a potentially fruitful explanation of differences in leadership. The transformational leadership model has been the theoretical framework for a number of leadership studies in organizational settings. Major findings from this research support the validity of the leadership theories proposed by Burns (1978) and Bass (1985a).

Bass (1985b) generated his theory of transformational leadership from data gathered in two exploratory studies. In his initial pilot study, Bass asked 70 senior executives to respond to an open-ended survey dealing with transformational leaders they had encountered in their careers. Subjects provided detailed descriptions of transformational leaders they had identified. Data analysis revealed some common characteristics of transformational leaders, which resulted in a strong sense of commitment among their followers.

Bass (1985b) developed a 73-item questionnaire based on the responses from his pilot study. In a second study, 176 senior U.S. Army officers completed the instrument. The results were factor-analyzed using principal components analysis. Two transactional factors and three transformational factors emerged. These five factors formulate the leadership dimensions described in Bass's model (1985b). The factor structure has been supported with further replications by Bass (1985b).

Avolio and Bass (1987) have revised the preliminary instrument in developing the Multifactor Leadership Questionnaire (MLQ), which is currently used to measure transactional and transformational leadership. Coefficient alpha estimates of reliability, based on responses from 728 subjects, range from 0.67 to 0.88 for the five subscales. Bass and Avolio (1990) have proposed that the MLQ can be used for selection, transfer, and promotion activities as well as individual, group, and organizational development.

Several investigations have been conducted that support hypotheses derived from transformational leadership theory. Bass (1985b) found that transformational factors were more highly correlated with perceived group effectiveness and job satisfaction than were transactional factors. Similar results on the effectiveness of transformational leaders were obtained in additional studies (Avolio, Waldman, & Einstein, 1988; Bass, Avolio, & Goodheim, 1987; Deluga, 1988). Transformational leadership was found to contribute more to individual performance and motivation than did transactional leadership (Waldman, Bass & Einstein, 1987). Research by Hater and Bass (1988) utilized superiors' ratings as well as subordinates' perceptions of transformational leaders. This study supports the augmentation effect of transformational leadership over transactional leadership on subordinate performance, satisfaction, and motivation. A cascading effect of transformational leadership was found in a study of two levels of management (Bass, Waldman, Avolio, & Bebb, 1987). Transformational leadership identified at one level of management was significantly correlated with the presence of perceived transformational leadership at the level immediately below.

Bennis and Nanus (1985) conducted in-depth interviews of 60 successful leaders in the public and private sectors. Analysis of the themes of the interviews revealed four leadership strategies common to effective leaders:

1. Attention through vision
2. Meaning through communication
3. Trust through positioning, and
4. Deployment of self through positive self-regard and optimism about a desired outcome

A vision is an image of a potential; it implies anticipation. A well-articulated vision provides a focus for members of an organization at all levels. Without a vision of the future, action has no direction. The role of the leader is to analyze the past and present to formulate a comprehensive view of the possible.

Communication of the vision must go beyond the verbal level. Nonverbal behavior that demonstrates the leader's commitment to the vision is a powerful means of conveying the significance of the mission. Bennis and Nanus (1985) call this the management of meaning. The leader shapes the way an organization works by institutionalizing the vision at all levels.

Positioning is "the set of actions necessary to implement the vision of the leader" (Bennis & Nanus, 1985, p. 46). The leader accomplishes this through carefully reacting to change, promoting change in the internal and/or external environments, and establishing a linkage between the internal and external environments. This promotes trust by clarifying and crystallizing the vision in relation to the environment. Followers perceive consistency and congruency in the leader's vision, which reduces ambiguity and resistance to change.

The final strategy suggested by Bennis and Nanus' findings (1985) is deployment of self. Deployment of self involves knowing and understanding one's strengths and weaknesses. This insight by the leader occurs on both the personal and organizational level. Self-knowledge that acknowledges strengths and compensates for weaknesses promotes confidence and optimism about the desired outcome.

The transformational leader empowers others to attain the vision. Bennis and Nanus (1985) identify four dimensions of empowerment: significance, competence, community, and enjoyment. Empowerment of followers, which creates the atmosphere necessary to achieve organizational excellence, is the outcome of effective transformational leadership.

Tichy and Devanna (1986) analyzed the process of organizational transformation. They interviewed 12 corporate leaders who were instrumental in initiating organizational change, and they discovered three steps that occur in organizational change.

The first phase of change in any organization is the identification of the need for change. This recognition results in response to events triggered by the environment. Astute leaders are sensitive to the dynamics for change yet are also alert to the forces within the organization that are resistant to change. The transformational leader creates a mood for revitalization within the organization by challenging the current institutional practices. This frame of mind provides the impetus for change to occur.

The second step in institutional change is creating a new vision. The transformational leader must communicate a vision that inspires others to let go of the past. It is important that the leader avoid the temptation to seek a quick-fix solution to the perceived organizational problems. A transformational vision is comprehensive in scope and involves long-term, qualitative change—individually and collectively.

The final stage of the transformational process is institutionalizing change. This phase requires a total restructuring of the organization. The leader acts as a social architect to realign technical, political, and cultural networks. Through the restructuring of the communication channels, the leader redirects the flow of information and influence to facilitate implementing change.

☐ *Implications for Nursing*

Transformational leadership theory provides a useful model for effective nursing leadership in modern health care settings. Transformational leadership is not a set of management techniques. It is a relationship grounded on the leader's values. At a time of crisis, Lee Iacocca, a familiar example of transformational leadership, communicated a vision that dramatically changed an entire corporation. The current crises in our nation's health care system also requires visionary leadership from the nursing profession.

Marshall Sashkin (1986) offers some suggestions on how to become a visionary leader. The ability to create a vision encompasses four cognitive skills. The first requires understanding the steps necessary to make a vision real. This skill, which Sashkin (1986) calls expressing the vision, includes strategic planning for implementing a change. Explaining the vision and the plan for action is the second critical component of visioning. Extending the vision to all parts of an organization is the third action of the visionary leader. The fourth skill is expanding the vision so that its message permeates the entire organizational culture. Creating a vision demands sharing ownership of the vision with the group and is focused on empowering others to carry out the vision (Sashkin, 1988).

The need for transformational leadership in nursing has never been greater. Transformational leadership is risky business. Commitment requires placing one's personal values on the line. However, the potential rewards to the nurse for this effort are great. The challenge of bringing about change at a higher level — transformation — exists today in nursing as never before for those willing to accept it.

□ *Application to Nursing: Case Study*

The dean of a school of nursing at a medium-sized state university in the Midwest has been in her current position for two years, following 20 years of teaching at several large universities. The majority of the faculty of the school are doctorally prepared, although most have only recently received their degrees (i.e., within the past five years).

One of the dean's goals is to increase scholarly activity and faculty research within the school. During the first two years of her administration, the dean has analyzed the factors that support and inhibit faculty participation in research. She found that the university administration is supportive of faculty research but that internal budgetary allocation for faculty research was limited. She believes that the nursing faculty value nursing research but perceive there is a lack of expertise and time to pursue scholarly activities.

At the nursing faculty workshop held at the beginning of the current academic year, the dean delivered her keynote address entitled "Research: The Key to Nursing Excellence." Each faculty member received a small metal key as a symbol of the theme. In addition, all correspondence to the faculty from the dean included the theme at the top of the page.

The dean established a strategic planning committee for research development consisting of faculty at all levels. She regularly attended the informal meetings of the research interest group established by recommendation of the planning committee. She requested and was granted a budget allotment from the university to hire outside consultants in research design and grant application. In the spring, the school sponsored a research symposium with a nationally known nurse researcher as the keynote speaker. All faculty attended a reception for the speaker hosted by the dean, where each was personally introduced to the speaker.

Questions for Discussion

1. What characteristics of charismatic leadership did the dean display?
2. How did the dean communicate her vision to the faculty?
3. Describe the empowerment strategies used by the dean in this situation.

4. What additional changes in the internal and external environment may be necessary for organizational transformation to occur?

References

Avolio, B.J. & Bass, B.M. (1987). Transformational leadership, charisma, and beyond. In J.G. Hunt, B.R. Baliga, H.P. Dachler, & C.A. Schriesheim (Eds.), *Emerging Leadership Vistas* (pp. 29-49). Lexington, KY: D.C. Heath.

Avolio, B.J., Waldman, D.A., & Einstein, W.O. (1988). Transformational leadership in a management game simulation: Impacting the bottom line. *Group and Organizational Studies, 1,* 59-80.

Bass, B.M. (1985a). *Leadership and performance beyond expectations.* New York: The Free Press.

Bass, B.M. (1985b). Leadership: Good, better, best. *Organizational Dynamics, 13* (3), 26-40.

Bass, B.M. & Avolio, B.J. (1990). *Manual for the Multifactor Leadership Questionnaire (MLQ).* Palo Alto, Calif.: Consulting Psychologists Press.

Bass, B.M., Avolio, B.J., & Goodheim, L. (1987). Biography and assessment of transformational leadership at the world-class level. *Journal of Management, 1,* 7-19.

Bass, B.M., Waldman, D.A., Avolio, B.J. & Bebb, M. (1987). Transformational leadership and the falling dominoes effect. *Group and Organizational Studies, 1,* 73-87.

Bennis, W. & Nanus, B. (1985). *Leaders: The strategies for taking charge.* New York: Harper & Row.

Bradley, R.T. (1987). *Charisma and social structure: A study of love and power, wholeness and transformation.* New York: Paragon House.

Burns, J.M. (1978). *Leadership.* New York: Harper & Row.

Conger, J.A. (1989). *The charismatic leader: Behind the mystique of exceptional leadership.* San Francisco: Jossey-Bass.

Conger, J.A. & Kanungo, R.N. (1987). Towards a behavioral theory of charismatic leadership in organizational settings. *Academy of Management Review, 12,* 637-647.

Conger, J.A. & Kanungo, R.N. (1988). Behavioral dimensions of charismatic leadership. In J.A. Conger, R.N. Kanungo, & Associates (Eds.), *Charismatic leadership: The elusive factor in organizational effectiveness* (pp. 78-97). San Francisco: Jossey-Bass.

Deluga, R.J. (1988). Relationship of transformational and transactional leadership with employee influencing strategies. *Group and Organizational Studies, 4,* 456-467.

Dow, T.E., Jr., (1969). The theory of charisma. *Sociological Quarterly, 10,* 306-318.

Hater, J.J. & Bass, B.M. (1988). Superiors' evaluations and subordinates' perceptions of transformational and transactional leadership. *Journal of Applied Psychology, 4,* 695-702.

House, R.J. (1977). A 1976 theory of charismatic leadership. In J. G. Hunt & L.L. Larson (Eds.), *Leadership: The cutting edge* (pp. 189-207). Carbondale, Ill.: Southern Illinois University Press.

Kegan, R. (1982). *The evolving self: Problem and process in human development.* Cambridge, Mass.: Harvard University Press.

Kuhnert, K.W. & Lewis, P. (1987). Transactional and transformational leadership: A constructive/developmental analysis. *Academy of Management Review, 4,* 648-657.

Sashkin, M. (1986). *Becoming a visionary leader: A guide for understanding and developing visionary leadership.* Bryn Mawr, Penn.: Organization Design and Development.

Sashkin, M. (1988). The visionary leader. In J.A. Conger, R.N. Kanungo, & Associates (Eds.), *Charismatic leadership: The elusive factor in organizational effectiveness* (pp. 122-160). San Francisco: Jossey-Bass.

Schweitzer, A. (1984). *The age of charisma.* Chicago: Nelson-Hall.

Tichy, N.M. & Devanna, M.A. (1986). *The transformational leader.* New York: John Wiley & Sons.

Trice, H.M. & Beyer, J.M. (1986). Charisma and its routinization in two social movement organizations. *Research in Organizational Behavior, 8,* 113-164.

Waldman, D.A., Bass, B.M., & Einstein, W.O. (1987). Leadership and outcomes of performance appraisal. *Journal of Occupational Psychology, 60,* 177-186.

Weber, M. (1947). *The theory of social and economic organization.* (A.M. Henderson & T. Parsons, Trans.). New York: Oxford University Press.

Willner, A.R. (1984). *The spellbinders: Charismatic political leadership.* New Haven, Conn.: Yale University Press.

II

Meaning Through Communication

3

KAY JACKSON-FRANKL

Management of Meaning

CHAPTER OBJECTIVES

□ Discuss the general role of language in the
  development and expression of meaning.

□ Describe organizational symbolism and its
  role in transformational leadership.

□ Define the concepts of meaning, language,
  symbols, and transformational leadership.

□ Apply these concepts to current nursing
  practice.

□ Evaluate the role of the leader in creating and
  communicating meaning.

The title of an article in a major business journal reads, "WANTED: Leaders who can make a difference" (Main, 1987, p. 92). Although this particular article is several years old, the message remains current. Leaders must make change happen. Business executives in fields ranging from health care to industry are facing challenges to the modus operandi of traditional organizations. Things that "aren't broke" are being evaluated for "fixing." Total quality management teams and the commitment to continual process and system improvements are emerging within organizations as American business leaders attempt to parallel the accomplishments of the Japanese. Crisis management and long-term planning are no longer the pivotal leadership characteristics. In addition, a leader must communicate a culture, inspire ownership in work, and motivate others toward personal and professional goals.

Fortunately, there are pioneers in this evolutionary process. Lee Iacocca, Tom Peters, Jack Welch, and John Reed exemplify a new executive breed called the "transformational leader." And though their particular industries and leadership styles may vary, one thing is in common among them: all manage meaning.

The management of meaning by leaders is the focus of this chapter. There is an assumption that leadership is an influence process in which the leader frames the reality of those who follow (Smirich and Morgan, 1982). This influence process is facilitated when the leader shares a language in common with the followers. A shared language enables the leader to communicate change through the use of familiar words. Words then become symbols depicting the present and future course of an organization. Thus the corporate vision can become a corporate reality.

Leaders who actively manage meaning for the purpose of changing reality are called transformational leaders. Like the mythical phoenix, a transformational leader creates new realities from the ashes of old meanings. Transformational leaders manage meaning; that is, they root a desired new vision in familiar meanings. Bass, Avolio, and Goodheim (1987) state that transformational leadership is ineffective if the leader cannot manage general operations. It is assumed that the transformational leader knows where the organization is going and is able to control the processes necessary to get there.

Another assumption of transformational leadership is that a transformational leader subscribes to the belief that all knowledge and meaning is subjective and can be created and shared. Meaning is idiosyncratically developed and defined and is rooted in the context of a particular person (Gray, Bougon, Donnellon, 1985). Each person shapes meaning within the context of lived experiences. These experiences may or may not be at the level of conscious recognition. Because each individual, including members of the same family, have developed personal conceptual structures, the meanings for experienced events are framed within the personal experience and are subjective. The task of the transformational leader is to reach the personal context of the follower.

The Meaning of Meaning: An Overview

It is beyond the scope of this chapter to provide a detailed discussion of meaning. The purpose of this overview is to acquaint the reader with the fundamentals of the concept of meaning and then explore meaning as it relates to organizational life.

A meaning is an individual reality. A meaning is an interpretation of an experienced life event. The experienced event may or may not be at a conscious level. Life events often involve interaction with other individuals. The human race is social, and humans tend to gravitate toward interactions with one another. As a person scrutinizes new interactions, understanding is sought for what has been experienced. Understanding, or interpretation, is a process whereby the experienced interaction is compared and contrasted with the person's known and unknown cognitive reality (Daft and Weick, 1983; Dubin, 1982; Gray, Bougon, and Donnellon, 1985). The unfamiliar is inspected for familiar and recognized patterns. An attempt is made to answer the question, "What is this interaction saying to me and how does it fit with what I already know?" Recognized patterns are used to place an experience within a particular relationship category. Closer scrutiny will determine if the new experience fits the existing category or if a new category must be established. According to Taylor (1985, p. 230), "A word only has the meaning it does in our lexicon because of what it contrasts with. What would red mean if we had no other colour terms? How would our colour terms change if some of our present ones dropped out?" Meanings arise as products of these interactions.

Meanings exist through language. When the language surrounding an experience is understood, meaning can be created. For example, consider the interactions involved in buying one's first personal computer. The sales representative methodically reviews the features and components of the system, spewing out the language associated with computers: disk drive, hard disk, floppy disk, terminal, monitor, megabytes, and so on. To the sales representative, the meaning of all this language is clear. The pattern concerning the interaction of all the objects make sense. There is an apparent order in the system. However, for the first-time purchaser, the apparent order may be lacking because the language is foreign. Perhaps the person has had no prior experience with the objects and the language. There is no "computer" relationship category in the person's knowledge base. For this new experience to have meaning, the objects, language, and associated interactions must become part of the person's familiar patterns; i.e., the person must associate the new experience with what is already known. In addition, the experience must be important to the person. An experience has meaning when it is important enough for a person to recognize the presence of the experience (Gray, Bougon, and Donnellon, 1985). This recognition can be at a conscious or preconscious level of cognition and requires the process of valuing (Epstein, 1983) or the connecting of the experience to things already known.

For the transformational leader, the valuing process is vital. The transformational leader is responsible for establishing connecting links between the potential followers and the direction of the organization. It is not enough to have a mission statement and a compulsory listing of operational values. Many if not all organizations have these components and people who can regurgitate their contents. The transformational leader accepts responsibility for analyzing how the vision will interact with all facets of the organization and then gives purposeful direction to the other leaders within the organization for successful implementation (Tichy and Ulrich, 1984). When implementing the vision, congruency among the leaders is crucial. The transformational leader must continually assess and reestablish the harmony of the vision.

Language as the Expression of Meaning

Language is synergistic: it is more than the sum of its parts. All forms of language, such as dance, music, poetry, art, and speech, contain symbols that express a person's understanding of and relationship with the world. Words need not be characters printed on paper. Chosen "words," whether spoken words, colors, or movements, are not random selections; rather, they are deliberate decisions simultaneously representing the known and unknown aspects of the speaker. "Conscious speech is like the tip of the iceberg. Much of what is going on in shaping our activity is not in our purview. Our deployment of language reposes on much that is preconscious and unconscious" (Taylor, 1985, p. 232).

Language enables a person to absorb the environment and to classify, categorize, and utilize the knowledge in various situations. The constructed meaning is framed by language and expressed through words chosen by the speaker. Language imposes dynamic patterns and categories that shape a person's reality. A frequently used example for illustrating this point is the Eskimos' use of 25 different words for "snow" (Nordland, 1988). If one does not understand these snow categories, one will not be able to see them. It would be necessary to expand one's snow vocabulary to communicate with the Eskimo about the snow. The meanings shaped through this process of understanding are dynamic because they are ever-changing with the introduction of new and unfamiliar experiences. The patterns that evolve are bounded only by the self-imposed limits of a person's cognitive reality.

Unfortunately, people do not process experiences completely or precisely. Instead, they process experiences according to held values. Language is processed only in pieces, and the relationships among these pieces are summarized and abstracted for the overall concept or gist (Daft and Wiginton, 1979). Therefore the information surrounding an experience represents pieces of conversation and personal understanding. It is the leader's responsibility to set the context for a shared vision through the use of words that capture the abstracted information being shared by the followers. Language that is too simple or too precise may lack the ability to capture and transmit the desired vision to a variety of people. Daft and Wiginton (1979) commented that leaders must have mastery of a "high variety language" and must recognize words as being one of the tools necessary for communicating a shared vision.

Language is an organization's lifeline: it both constitutes and sustains the organizational community. Events, issues, crises, and commodities have their meanings for the people of an organization because of its language. It is not possible to understand an organization without understanding its language. Try to imagine an organization in which everyone spoke a different language but had to produce a common output. The task would be quite arduous, ineffective, and inefficient. Language focuses a person on what is internally and externally valued by an organization.

Boje, Fedor, and Rowland (1982) stated, "Language not only determines what we see, but how we interpret what we see." The organization's culture is transmitted via its language, and transformational leaders are knowledgeable about both. Organizations are collections of people experiencing social interactions and identifying with a collective "we" (Harris and Cronen, 1979). The ability to survive, belong, and prosper within an organization requires an understanding of its culture. Most individuals receive their introduction to the culture during orientation and introductory periods. During this time, various leaders, both formal and informal, transmit organizational assumptions, values, and beliefs through the careful selection of words symbolizing the organization's culture. It is crucial that these leaders relate the culture with a harmonious language. The presence of disharmony in the shared vision creates a fragmented corporate culture. A dramatic example of the need for harmonious language is seen in the orientation to the armed services. Evered (1983) provided a very detailed discussion of the language that must be quickly mastered by a Navy recruit. The inability of the recruit to achieve familiarity with the new language may hold both personal and global consequences.

However, because meanings are personally constructed realities, there is no guarantee that meanings are accurate (Dubin, 1982). Indeed, even when a common language is spoken, there is no guarantee that the meaning is shared. Jackson-Frankl (1989) interviewed 15 members of a nursing staff practicing in a large midwestern university hospital. The randomly selected nurses included staff nurses, head nurses, and nurse administrators, as well as the vice president of nursing. All were asked to describe what the words "quality," "care," and "quality of care" meant to them. While themes of meaning for each word were present within each of the three groups, the themes were not consistently shared either within or between the groups. Yet the organization was able to exist and progress because the individuals shared an understanding about the role of the organization (health care) and their active roles within it (health care providers). These actions and meanings are not separable (Weick, 1969). There is a mutual construction of meaning among the members of an organization concerning roles and the expected outcomes. What is expressed through language is the meaning these events have for the organization's people.

Leaders, Language, and Meaning

Pondy (1978, p. 87) defined leadership as the "ability to use social or interpersonal influence over a subordinate." Influence is a power that indirectly or intangibly affects a person or a course of events. The ability to influence another is related to the ability to speak the other's language. According to Morris (1949, p. 214), "Sharing a language provides the subtlest and most powerful tool for controlling the behavior of . . . other persons to one's advantage." However, influencing and motivating others to action requires at least two additional things: first, the leader must make sense of what needs to be done; and second, the leader must put it into words so that the meaning of the action becomes real and can be accomplished.

A transformational leader creates comfort with ambiguity and maintains a vision of rationality in an irrational world. Rationality is maintained when the new and unfamiliar is cloaked in the words of the known and familiar. Pondy and Huff (1985) studied the process of integrating microcomputers into an elementary and junior high school system. This integration represented a fundamental change to the system, yet it transpired quite smoothly because the leader in charge of the project rooted the unfamiliar in the familiar. The regular meetings of the Board of Education were used to introduce the topic. Articles and handouts were prepared that discussed the computer as the "ultimate audio-visual machine" (p. 109) and computer literacy as a "basic skill" (p. 111). In this way, the introduction of the computers was framed as an extension of the known, rather than as the introduction of unfamiliar objects.

Leaders emerge because of their ability to communicate a vision meaningfully. Even in "leaderless" groups, certain individuals emerge as being prominent because of their ability to define the situation and guide the necessary actions. The "followers" then look to the leaders for guidance as they define their role in the vision. Thus the leader must be able to articulate the vision in a meaningful way but must also make the vision operational through appropriately chosen actions.

Making a vision operational requires "moxie." Dubin (1982) defined moxie as having the energy to move in "high gear" and the ability to be creative in understanding organizations. Lee Iacocca's development of the Chrysler campaign is an example of moxie in action. Iacocca (1984) frequently asserted that the financial situation at Chrysler was not an isolated case but that other car companies, namely Ford and GM, would also soon have difficulties. Iacocca (1984) chose a language combination that established Chrysler as a symbol that transformed how people within and outside the corporation saw the company's situation. The company still had to produce, but through the symbolization process "it created a situation in which it could perform. It created a situation that would not have existed if it had not spoken out about problems and solutions" (Mann, 1988, p. 22).

Organizations are complex systems of individuals who use and interpret language, develop meaning, and thereby create their own reality. Thus, if reality is socially constructed (Berger and Luckman, 1966), then one of the defining characteristics of organizations is that within an organization there are shared definitions of the world (Pfeffer, 1981). A definition is an interpretation. A critical element in forming a definition is the sharing of information among and between leaders and followers. Organizations remain organized so long as the leaders maintain coherence when communicating interpretations. Shared interpretations preserve the structure of the organization. Thus, though it is not necessary for everyone to agree on an interpretation, leaders must harmoniously communicate the interpretation so it is congruent when communicated to others.

Counterreality results when individuals hold different meanings that result in different actions. In contrast, an equifinal meaning is one in which the interpretations differ but the end result does not. Counterrealities and equifinal meanings are important concepts in the "construction and destruction" of meaning (Gray et al., 1985).

As an example, Smirich (1983) explored the effects of words used by top management within an insurance company. The company was having a particularly difficult period and the executive group was desperately trying to pull the management staff together. Top management developed a "Wheeling Together" theme, in which the spokes of the wheel represented the various individuals who needed to work together to produce the desired results.

Unfortunately, counterrealities resulted because the language was not shared. Various negative interpretations resulted because the staff was not involved and the context surrounding the theme was one of secrecy and distrust. As stated before, managing meaning is holistic: it is the total process of creating a purposeful, visionary, corporate culture.

Organizational Symbolism

To manage meaning is to impart the practice of organizational symbolism. Organizational symbolism is the study of language, metaphors, myths, and other symbols within organizations. A core premise of organizational symbolism is that organizations do not function on the traditional mechanistic model. People are not machines. They require more than fuel and a structured, routine job on an assembly line. Organizational symbolism is a challenge to the paradigm that values the rational action of individuals and organizations. The ontological commitment (belief system) of organizational symbolism focuses on the individual's creation of meaning and reality through social interaction.

A symbol is a meaning that goes beyond the obvious empirical findings. Within business the classic example is the gold watch presented at retirement. For some individuals the gold watch is no more than a watch. But to others, the gold watch stands for years of hard work and achievement within an organization.

Symbols and the process of symbolization are vital components of transformational leadership. When leaders use language that has meaning for the follower, they are using symbolization to establish a vision for followers. To the degree that the vision is shared, so will be the effectiveness of any actions. Leaders must be able to utilize symbols effectively and efficiently so that the behaviors necessary for a task or for a change in task can be defined, established, and placed within the organization's routines. The presence of multiple meanings, without a shared perspective concerning expectations, can result in ambiguity and discontent.

Shared or coincident meanings (Gray et al., 1985) are created. Shared experiences are maintained through repeated interactions so that the experiences come to have a common meaning. According to Pfeffer (1981, p. 14), "shared understandings are likely to emerge to rationalize the patterns of behavior that develop, and in the absence of such rationalization and meaning creation, the structured patterns of behavior are likely to be less stable and persistent."

Transformational leaders encourage shared meanings through symbolic speech. Symbolic speech is persuasive speech. The use of symbols by leaders reestablishes the importance of imaginative thought and action in organizational life. For example, one midwestern health care system gives suspenders to individuals when they are "caught upholding the mission." This recognized individual wears the suspenders until he or she "catches" someone else exhibiting mission behaviors. The set of meanings that arises from the use of such symbols comes to portray the distinctive character of the group, which is then shared and sustained through language, rituals, and myths (Pondy et al, 1983).

A metaphor is a representation that describes something through the use of an unrelated object. A metaphor describes with an "as if" quality by transferring meaning for one object to another. Lakoff and Johnson (1980) stated that the metaphor has a special role in the development of understanding for how events are framed. For example, the description that someone is "cold as ice" provides an instant picture of how that person is seen. In the same way, organizational metaphors provide information about the ways in which people within the organization frame organizational events. In the earlier example, the suspenders are a metaphor symbolizing valued behaviors.

Organizations are rich in metaphors. Hirsch and Andrews (1983) studied the organizational takeover phenomenon and classified the language as representing either friendly or hostile takeovers. Hostile takeovers were characterized by military metaphors. There were "sieges" and "ambushes," with "battles" and "mankillers." The "enemy" was often in "hot pursuit." In contrast, friendly takeovers were described by "cavalier" metaphors such as "white knights" and "saviors." Hirsch and Andrews (1983) proposed that the use of such language provides a buffer that distances those involved from the stress surrounding the events. In any case, the metaphors provide graphic insights into how the affected individuals are understanding the event.

Smith and Simmons (1983) also provided a detailed description of an organizational metaphor. A psychoeducational facility that will be referred to as Dexter was preparing to open. The facility, for emotionally disturbed children and adults, required 15 years of planning among various state and county agencies. While all the agencies shared the common goal of opening Dexter, they conflicted on how the facility would operate. None of these conflicts were resolved before Dexter opened. The turmoil resulted in Dexter being described with the "Rumplestiltskin" metaphor. Initially the leader, played by the gnome, attempted to create and deliver the promised Dexter program. However budget cuts and sacrifices, represented by the daughter's promise of the firstborn to the gnome, brought hardship to the program. When the staff realized that they could not deliver the program, they chose a scapegoat, firing the leader. According to the researchers, "much of the power of the Rumplestiltskin tale at Dexter was that it provided signposts to the relationships between the manifest and the unconscious" (p. 391). "Signs" that were visible were the years of planning and the unrelenting conflicts. These conflicts developed a pattern (the unconscious) that resembled the Rumplestiltskin tale. Recognizing this metaphorical pattern would assist a leader to move the corporation toward resolution of the longstanding conflicts.

Metaphors are examples of "abstract concepts giv[ing] meaning and structure to the [individuals'] psychological reality" (Astley, 1985, p. 501). Weick (1988) commented that the most common metaphor in business is the military metaphor. He hypothesized that this kind of metaphor is so prevalent because the need for order is so prevalent. "People don't like to deal with uncertainty and disorder so they impose military trappings like hierarchies and spans of control to conceal the disorder. Military imagery probably also exists because it is tough, macho, exciting" (p. 3). His alternative was to "think of your organization as an octopus."

Conceptualizing an organization as an octopus takes creative energy. It is a new and different thought. The conceptualization of an organization as a military establishment takes little or no creative energy because it is a familiar metaphor. Transformational leaders, leaders who dare to change organizations, must also dare to change the dominant metaphor. And if the octopus does not work, what about a coral cluster? "Different metaphors can constitute and capture the nature of organizational life in different ways, each generating powerful, distinctive, but essentially partial kinds of insight . . . new metaphors may be used to create ways of viewing organizations which overcome the weaknesses . . . of traditional metaphors . . ." (Morgan, 1980, p. 612).

Boland and Pondy (1983) studied accounting as a metaphor in how organizations respond to the environment. The organization they studied was a university whose formal budget process has developed over the past 50 years. Each cycle took over two years to complete and was extremely structured and steeped in tradition. The university was held in high esteem by the state, and over the past 10 years it received a large share of the available state dollars. But enrollment began to decline and budget cuts were needed. The operational values of the budget process were questioned. The traditional way of allocating funds no longer made sense to the involved individuals because the context of the situation had changed. The new problem was how to make sense of the changes in environments, both internal and external, and how to establish a meaningful new reality. In this situation, the key administrators held special meetings with the faculty and attended regular faculty meetings. The meanings of the budget categories were gradually altered to accommodate the new environment. "Transcending the formal accounting system does not come easy and requires an act of courage. When we think of accounting as strictly rational it is hard to see this need for transcendence and courage. It becomes apparent only as we appreciate the natural system aspect of accounting through the lived experience of the individual" (p. 230).

Manning (1979) also explored organizational metaphors. The context for this study was a police department. Manning developed the metaphor "Master Detective" after exploring the words used by police personnel to frame their policing and detective roles. Examples of their terminology included "working informant," "beefs" (arrests), "narcs," and "making a case." The interactions between and among these references shaped the reality of those employed by the department. A different reality would have existed if the metaphor had been different. For example, what if a boxing metaphor had been used? The "narcs" might be "champs" and the "informants" "opponents to win." The message is that metaphors can be used to develop and transmit the organizational reality to others. Metaphors play a significant role in the transformation of organizations. To create a phoenix requires a strong vision and persuasive language.

Persuasive language is a learned art. "It is not a manipulative endeavor, it is an educational process for you and your intended receiver" (Blake, 1987, p. 49). The assumption in persuasion is that the persuader, the leader, knows where to go and has some clear ideas of how to get there. Successful persuasion, like successful leadership, rests on effective decisions. Persuasion is creative decision making and requires leaders with moxie. Iacocca used persuasion, as did Reed of Citicorp. Persuasion is the active and conscious use of symbols to generate understanding and motivation in others.

☐ *Implications for Nursing*

Leadership as management of meaning has been the focus of this chapter. Language and meaning have been discussed and the role of the leader in shaping and communicating a meaningful vision to followers was explained.

The successful nursing leader manages meaning through hard work. There are no prescriptive methods for developing persuasive speech and motivating symbols. The aforementioned individuals are examples of transformational leaders who immersed themselves in their businesses and who understood the underlying spirit of their businesses. Managing meaning is the leader's responsibility. It cannot be delegated. Each nursing leader must create a personally comfortable style for establishing and sharing the corporate vision.

Part of the process for sharing the vision is understanding the followers' perception of the current situation. Transformational nursing leaders do not assume that those individuals who do similar work share a common language. Instead, these leaders seek verbalized shared goals and then translate these goals into shared symbols.

Transformational nursing leaders have clearly defined corporate visions. The significant corporate concepts are identified, and the vision is expressed in logical and meaningful ways. Expectations are clearly articulated and reinforced. There are elements of fun, creativity, and self-worth in the language used by the nursing leaders and followers. Things make sense because the vision is one that is understood and shared by all, with everyone having an essential part in its continuous development.

The language of the nursing leader is in constant concert with the vision, and everyone is responsible for understanding and sharing the vision in harmony with the leader. New people are told about the corporate vision and their responsibilities in that vision on the first day of orientation and are provided with a positive opportunity to leave if these new ideas are not what they desire. Dynamic congruency is essential for a thriving vision and culture.

❑ *Application to Nursing: Case Study*

Metro Memorial is a multifacility system in the Midwest. The system includes two acute care medical-surgical hospitals, one acute care mental health facility, and two long-term care facilities (one is a private facility and the other a state facility). Each facility is no more than 8 miles from another member facility. However, there are numerous other health care facilities within a 15-minute ride from any facility in the system. All together, the system employs over 3,500 people.

The system was established through four separate mergers. Two old medical-surgical hospitals merged into one new facility approximately 10 years ago. The new hospital then merged with another medical-surgical hospital, but each hospital kept its own name and identity. Another merger brought the mental health facility into the system, and a final merger included the long-term care facilities.

During the past 15 months the system has lost two vice presidents (VPs) of nursing, one chief executive officer (CEO), one chief operating officer (COO), and several middle managers and staff. Recruitment and retention are difficult because the community perceives the system as unstable and unreliable. It was also found through exit interviews and focus surveys that long-term employees and the community are still mourning over the original merger, 10 years ago, of the two old hospitals. Market share has dropped, and patient census is falling.

A new CEO and VP of nursing have arrived and wish to change the internal and external perceptions of the system. Open communication and a strong emphasis on visible leadership have been key components of the new executive staff. Unfortunately, each facility is still not recognizing that it is part of a team system. Rumors about layoffs and an uncaring administration are being found in the system and the community. And just yesterday the CEO announced that beginning in January the Total Quality Management process will begin to be implemented throughout the system. This process represents a philosophy very different from the organization's prevailing mode.

Questions for Discussion

1. List the top four crises affecting the system and discuss these crises using the concepts of language, meaning, symbols, and leadership as the framework for discussion.
2. Evaluate the role that the merger of the two old hospitals plays in the system's current situation. Look for the process of symbolization in the evaluation.
3. Given the CEO's commitment to Total Quality Management, create a strategic plan for optimal implementation. Consider the concepts outlined in the chapter. How would a transformational leader bring about this change? Hypothesize the outcome and support your decision.

References

Astley, G. (1985). Administrative science as socially constructed truth. *Administrative Science Quarterly, 30,* 497-513.

Bass, B.M. (1985). *Leadership and performance beyond expectations.* New York: The Free Press.

Bass, B.M., Avolio, B.J., and Goodheim, L. (1987). Biography and the assessment of transformational leadership at the world class level. *Journal of Management,* (January) 7-19.

Berger, P. and Luckman, T. (1966). *The social construction of reality: a treatise in the sociology of knowledge.* Garden City, N.Y.: Doubleday.

Blake, L. (1987). Communicate with clarity: manage meaning. *Personnel Journal,* 43-50.

Boje, D., Fedor, D., and Rowland, K. (1982). Myth making: a qualitative step into OD interventions. *Journal of Applied Behavioral Science, 18,* 17-28.

Boland, R. and Pondy, L. (1983). Accounting in organizations: a union of national and rational perspectives. *Accounting, Organizations and Society, 8,* 223-234.

Cassirer, E. (1944). *An essay on man.* New Haven, Conn.: Yale University Press.

Daft, R. and Weick, K. (1983). Toward a model of organizations as interpretation systems. *Academy of Management Review, 9,* 284-295.

Daft, R. and Wiginton, J. (1979). Language and organizations. *Academy of Management Review, 4,* 179-191.

Dubin, R. (1982). Management: meanings, methods, and moxie. *Academy of Management Review, 7,* 373-379.

Epstein, S. (1983). The unconscious, the preconscious, and the self-concept. In J. Sals and A. Greenwald (Eds.), *Psychological perspectives on the self: The role of the unconscious in an individual's selfsystem.* (Vol. 2, pp. 219-247). Hillsdale, N.J.: Lawrence Erlbaum and Associates.

Evered, R. (1983). The language of organizations: The case of the Navy. In L. Pondy, P. Frost, G. Morgan and T. Dandridge (Eds.), *Organizational Symbolism.* Greenwich, Conn.: JAI Press.

Gray, B., Bougon, M., and Donnellon, A. (1985). Organizations as constructions and destructions of meaning. *Journal of Management, 11,* 83-98.

Harris, L., and Cronen, V. (1979, Winter). A rules based model for the analysis and evaluation of organizational communication. *Communication Quarterly,* 12-38.

Hirsch, P., and Andrews, J. (1983). Ambushes, shootouts, and knights of the round table: the language of corporate takeovers. In L. Pondy, P. Frost, G. Morgan, and T. Dandridge (Eds.), *Organizational Symbolism.* Greenwich, Conn.: JAI Press.

Iacocca, L. (1984). *Iacocca.* New York: Bantam Books.

Jackson-Frankl, K. (1989). *Symbotics in Nursing Administration.* Unpublished doctoral dissertation, Indiana University School of Nursing.

Lakoff, G., and Johnson, M. (1980). *Metaphors we live by.* Chicago: University of Chicago Press.

Main, J. (1987, September). Wanted: leaders who make a difference. *Fortune,* 92-102.

Mann, C. (1988, Spring). Transformational leadership in the executive office. *Public Relations Quarterly,* 19-23.

Manning, P. (1979). Metaphors of the field: varieties of organizational discourse. *Administrative Science Quarterly, 24,* 660-671.

Morgan, G. (1980). Paradigms, metaphors, and puzzle solving in organizational theory. *Administrative Science Quarterly, 25,* 605-622.

Morris, C.W. (1949). *Signs, language and behavior.* New York: Prentice Hall.

Nordland, R. (1988, Spring). How to speak basic Baksheesh. In Ziegler, M. (Ed), *Trips* (1), p. 53.

Pfeffer, J. (1981). Management as symbolic action: the creation and maintenance of organizational paradigms. In L.L. Cummings, and B. Staw (Ed.), *Research in organizational behavior, 3,* 1-51. Greenwich, Conn.: JAI Press.

Pondy, L. (1978). Leadership is a language game. In M. McCall and M. Lombardo (Eds.), *Leadership: where else can we go?* 87-99. North Carolina: Duke University.

Pondy, L., Frost, P.J., Morgan, G., and Dandridge, T. (Eds.) (1983). *Organizational Symbolism.* Greenwich, Conn.: JAI Press.

Pondy, L., and Huff, A. (1985). Achieving routine in organizational change. *Journal of Management, 11,* 103-116.

Smirich, L. (1983). Organizations as shared meanings. In Pondy, L. et al. (Eds.), *Organizational symbolism.* Greenwich, Conn.: JAI Press.

Smirich, L., and Morgan, G. (1982). Leadership: the management of meaning. *The Journal of Applied Behavioral Science, 18,* 257-273.

Smith, K., and Simmons, V. (1983). A Rumpelstiltskin organization: metaphors on metaphors in field research. *Administrative Science Quarterly, 28,*377-392.

Taylor, C. (1985). *Human agency and language. Philosophical papers 1.* New York: Cambridge University Press.

Tichy, N., and Ulrich, D. (1984, Fall). SMR Forum: the leadership challenge—a call for the transformational leader. *Sloan Management Review,* 59-68.

Weick, K. E. (1969). *The social psychology of organizing.* Reading, Mass.: Addison-Wesley.

Weick, K. E. (1988). The metaphor of business. *Health Matrix, 6(2),* 2-4.

Trust Through Positioning

4

DIANA LUSKIN BIORDI

Ethical Leadership

CHAPTER OBJECTIVES

☐ Differentiate between teleological and deontological systems of ethics.

☐ Discuss the implications of gender on moral reasoning, especially in regard to health care professions.

☐ Interpret new trends in ethics discussions in light of health care trends.

☐ Compare likely nursing administrative ethical responses to likely non-nursing administrative responses to ethical issues and dilemmas.

☐ Forecast the expected ethical issues facing all administrators in health care in the next decade.

☐ Apply various principles of moral behavior to choices regarding health care issues or dilemmas, especially in regard to nursing administration.

We live in an Age of Information. Since the advent of this age 40 years ago, the nurse's work and social world have changed tumultuously. The old manufacturing economy has given way to one of service. Information is the capital of service; the management of information will not only be a necessity, but a paramount value. As a major resource, knowledge will provide nursing managers and practitioners opportunity, as well as predictability, in a changing health care system.

Although the movement toward service and information began in the affluence following World War II, the decade of the 1960s became the watershed of social change, when old-line authority structures were visibly and frequently breached. The breaches were accompanied by a profound reexamination of community and status. The reexamination has created a grand negotiation, still taking place, in our work worlds (with ripple effects upon the associated work arenas of home life and volunteerism). First to be examined was the status quo (beginning in the 1950s and 1960s). Then in the 1970s, power was examined: who had it; who should have it; and its bases, strategies, and effects. In the 1970s and 1980s, society began to broaden its definition of allowable players beyond white Anglo-Saxon men to include women, minorities, the old, and the young. Now in the 1980s and early 1990s, while we are still examining the qualifications of today's workers, we find the world in a new economy. Given all of these changes, we are beginning to reevaluate the rules of right behavior — ethics — by which we will govern ourselves in a workplace populated by diversity of workers and types of knowledge. In this new social era, with its rapidly changing work and behaviors, nurses and managers must make informed choices according to an acceptable standard of behavior and, insofar as possible, understand the implications of their choices.

In health care, the effects of the last 30 years have been clear. From a rather sleepy world of tight stratification and a kind of noblesse oblige, health care has been transformed from a privilege to an equal-distribution right. Recent changes in reimbursement and the impact of information have led to a market-driven model of care. In health care, as elsewhere in the economy, the market will prevail. This has led to hospital competition and diversification, multiagency systems, and the search for paying "consumers." It has forced formalized quality controls. It has created a client orientation and health care for the "me generation" of consumers. It is forcing health care out of hospitals and into homes. It is providing a two-tiered system of care, divided between the haves and have-nots. It has offered more opportunities to more workers (i.e., the literate, women, and minorities). It is leveling the solidarity and expertise of physicians while raising that of other health care workers. It argues for rationing of health care resources. And it has bankrupted the unresponsive.

Changing systems, values, economics, and demographics are the four major forces reforming health care today. These forces, as well as the rapidity of the changes, are unravelling the view of health care once commonly shared by health care workers and patients. In making new sense of health care changes, ethical rules of right behavior help keep health care workers, whatever their work role, on track.

Consistent with the range and impact of these reforming forces, however, a plurality of issues and ethical approaches in health care now exists. Unexamined health care decisions will probably perpetuate fluid or already confused situations. Once the underlying values and ethical linkages are made clear, an examined decision will more likely articulate better with other decisions. Nursing managers or practitioners will be in a more advantageous position to proceed in their work and negotiate a future if they can better understand and evaluate their decisions, current issues, and assumptions about major ethical systems.

Ethics

What do we mean by ethics? Ethics is basically a study of morality. At least three broad domains of ethics and morals exist: (1) the philosophy (and related theologies) of ethics; (2) the normative or moral interpretive view of behaviors (e.g., sociology); and (3) the everyday or popularist view. In health care organizations, as elsewhere, these three domains each relate to the following:

- Applications relating to the person or the community;
- The private or public display of the act;
- The colleagueship or hierarchy of the organizational relationships in question;
- The means or ends of the moral process;
- The freedom and good will with which decisions are made and judged.

Also, a tension exists between an abstract (what ought to be) and a real behavior (what is). This tension can be exacerbated because the development of moral reason and action is both individually and group constrained. For nurses and other health care workers, these tensions between the abstract good and real life are often brought out in the negotiations of salient health care issues (especially resource allocation) and moral dilemmas.

Ethics, as philosophy, represents the "oughts" of a code of behavior. The right or wrong, good or bad, of behavior is examined against certain criteria of morality. These criteria are themselves subject to study, whether in philosophy or other interpretive disciplines. However, ethics as a study of right and wrong behavior is specifically in the domain of philosophy (Curtin and Flaherty, 1982; Singer, 1961). Because ethics is largely concerned with how people should act, questions that follow concern the nature and limits of actions, the actors, and their relative autonomy in acting (moral agents). Some would also argue that ethics is a formal or explicit set of rules (Jameton, 1984). All of these questions can lead to inquiry of the nature of knowledge and reality, which is of interest to theorists of all disciplines. However, significant relationships exist between philosophy, on the one hand, and social sciences and professions — especially nursing, medicine, social work, political science, religion, psychology, and sociology — on the other. In all of these disciplines, conceptions of right and wrong actions and moral character are intricately related to dominant conceptions of practice models, governance, organizational life, and the relationships between individuals and their social or work groups. Ultimately, each discipline judges its work according to different criteria of competence within an occupational "moral order."

Insofar as they are separatists, some ethicists would argue that by their very analyses social scientists and practitioners are engaging in moral discourse philosophically separate from other disciplines. But without a very specific moral examination the separatist philosophers would further argue that the findings of the social scientists and practitioners are necessary but insufficient conditions for the development of morally right policies (Garner and Rosen, 1967). Nursing managers and practitioners who, in the course of defining and managing ethical concerns, come into contact with these philosophical notions then must make two judgements. The first is about the nature of the philosophers' separateness and its impact on the nurses' understanding. The second judgement is about the nature of the nurses' own, typically feminine, views of separateness.

Those disciplines that study the actual conduct examine real behaviors and their rationale. Sociology, for example, explicitly studies the "moral order" as developed and enacted by groups, whereas psychology and psychoanalysis examine real behaviors or feelings of individuals. From the examination of actual conduct, these disciplines offer descriptions, interpretations, and prescriptions of right behaviors as interpreted by the actors and the investigators.

In the inquiry into actual conduct and its study in ethics, there is an overlap with epistemology (knowledge development), the existentialist school of agency and decisions (responsible agents of choice), and the phenomenological approach that emphasizes the concrete data of moral experience. These areas of overlap can have important consequences for health care organizations. For example, the convening of an ethics committee may bring together members of several disciplines but exclude others. The question of who is accepted and who is disenfranchised will have serious implications for patient care and for health care workers in that organization (Edwards and Haddad, 1988). When nurses examine incident reports, which relate to nurses' work and the corporate meaning of nursing error (notions of right and wrong, good or bad), philosophy and epistemology overlap, but they also overlap with issues of governance. And when we examine governance, the leaders of nursing or health care organizations, reflecting the values of the corporate culture, are in the double position of being moral models (regarding what ought to be) and moral agents (what really is) for the organization (see Grier, 1989). How well a nursing leader transforms ideals — especially those of caring — into conduct is significant to patients, their nurses, the nursing profession, and the business of health care (Biordi, 1986; Fry, 1989; Jackall, 1988; Dunham, 1989; MacPherson, 1989; Reilly, 1989).

Nursing leaders must have well-developed personal ethics, which they consistently enact, and the ability to inspire their organizational followers toward the realization of corporate goals. Drucker (1966, p. 52) declared that "management without values, commitment, and convictions can only do harm." And Morford (1989) argued that leaders must clarify, know, and be ready to act upon their basic life values and their most basic professional values to solve the really difficult ethical dilemmas with courage and conviction. To clarify these values, the most profound question a leader can ask and answer is, "What would I die for?" (Morford, 1989). The answers to this question help establish personal integrity, the *sine qua non* of the genuine leader. Without integrity, trust is impossible. Without trust, all else eventually fails or is derailed (McCall and Lombardo, 1983; Schrock, 1980).

Ethical Principles, Reasoning, and Approaches

Principles and values that guide personal ethics are also examined in the study of ethics. Historically, these principles have raised questions about right, good, ought, justice, obligation, freedom, duty, reciprocity, and enforceability (Young and Hayne, 1988). These principles and their interconnections have been intellectually developed to determine whether any of them can transcend their context and be context-free, or universal. Recent writers, under the impetus of great social and technological change, have reconsidered ethics and subsequent principles, especially in light of previously unconsidered issues (e.g., the environment) and have derived other, important principles that guide ethical behavior. Some of these that remain critical to leadership will be discussed in the next sections.

In the decision-making process, whether in management or in other work, sooner or later one encounters a moral dilemma. The resolution of a dilemma may serve to clarify or make salient values between two mutually incompatible choices. Kohlberg (1984), using moral dilemmas as a research method and basing his work on the Piagetian theme of justice as the core of morality, developed a three-level/six-stage model (Omery, 1989, p. 503, 504). In the first level of Kohlberg's (1984) model, the development of *moral reasoning* in an individual moves from doing right first because of authority; second, out of fairness; and finally, because of immediate reciprocity for a long-term payoff. In the second level, *conventional reasoning,* moral reasoning moves from an egocentric to a societal perspective, first because one does right and looks right to others, and then because doing right is one's duty. The overriding reason is the fear of societal breakdown if everyone obeyed his or her own imperatives. In the third level, *principled reasoning,* moral reasoning moves from a perspective of societal to universal reasoning. In this level, the individual chooses to do right because of the cooperative networks that are maintained and, finally, because of the rational person's belief in and commitment to the validity of universal ethical principles and the greatest good for the many (Omery, 1989).

Kohlberg's (1984) model has been heavily criticized because he claims that women have been "arrested" at the third stage of the second level, *mutual morality* (where right is doing what is expected of them because there is a need to be perceived by others as good people). Although the majority of the population has been shown to be arrested at this level, more women than men were unable to move beyond this stage. In this case, the model suggests the moral superiority of men, since more men than women could move to higher levels.

Carol Gilligan (1982) questions the position of deviancy or arrest taken in Kohlberg's interpretation. She argues that feminine moral reasoning is simply different from masculine moral reasoning and that both men and women develop their moral reasoning in the context of social interaction. Because women and men are socialized differently, they might be expected to have relationships that bound their moral experience and, consequently, have different stages of moral reasoning (Omery, 1989). Gilligan (1982) notes the dependency and survival needs of women in a male-dominated world and argues that their moral reasoning is based on a sense of a universal responsibility to care in order to survive. Noddings (1984) also makes a philosophical case for caring, especially in response to the service industry of teaching. Both argue that the universal moral guide governing all moral reasoning becomes caring and that quite different but useful models evolve from this universal obligation.

Management Requirements and Ethics

These models of the development of moral reasoning have importance to the management of health care, not only because of their methodologies (using moral conflict) and different subsequent emphases (justice, caring), but because of the impact of their gender relationships to the worker pool in health care. Because all men do not follow Kohlberg's (1984) model and all women do not follow Gilligan's (1982), the assumptions of one model will have consequences that may not be fully understood by individuals who do not follow that line of moral reasoning. For example, although the health care work force is primarily women (e.g., 94% of nurses are women), it is dominated by men (90% of hospital CEOs are men) (Biordi, 1986). Moreover, the influx into health care of community-minded minorities, who are apt to hold traditional values of feminine-masculine relationships, is also likely to reinforce gender-related differences. If female health care workers subscribe to the Gilligan model and the male professionals and managers subscribe to the Kohlberg interpretation, the potential for conflict and moral dilemmas increases. Then if moral dilemmas that affect women (e.g., nurses) are addressed by male professionals and managers, it is quite likely that the solutions to the dilemmas will not have support among all professionals.

Indeed, the literature in nursing ethics is replete with the conflicts nurses feel when their voices are not heard in the care of patients. Yarling and McElmurry (1986, p. 65) in a now-classic article, go so far as to say that nurses "are not free to be moral because they are deprived of the free exercise of moral agency." It is especially important to remember that decisions made at one level of a hierarchy have profound implications for those who must implement such decisions. This is even more critical when the decision is made unilaterally and independently of the nurse implementor and where decision-making organizational hierarchies are shifting or fading. Theis (1986) makes the point to physicians that all members of the health care team should examine their values and better understand the processes of ethical decision making. "Emotional, intuitive unilateral responses to moral situations may do more harm than good" (Theis, 1986, p. 1124). For the manager, ethics in isolation creates unnecessary risk and potential harm to the patient and workers alike.

Management work has never been easy, given the many constituencies that must be served. In the Information Age, management has shifted dramatically: the greater complexity and interdependencies fostered by more constituencies and information have blurred the previously clear boundaries and hierarchies (Kanter, 1989). This change in the nature of work has been more obvious in industry than in health care. Nonetheless, because of the market-driven models, only banking has had more radical shifts in work boundaries and manager outplacement than nursing and health care (Jones, personal communication, May 1989).

Besides the shifting of boundaries, alliances, and jobs, the outlook for the future in health care management is in humanism. To stay competitive in the last decade managers had to face the consequences and merge, cut, or otherwise reshape management structures to be "leaner and meaner" (note the metaphor). Downsizing and cost-cutting were the rallying points. Often such managers did these things over objections and without regard to human autonomy and respect (Daley-Gawenda, et al., 1986). Now, after the actions have been taken, and in response to the changing intellectual and market climate, tough bosses are being replaced by people-oriented leaders who can speak to human values of trust, empathy, caring, and courage (Bennis, 1989). What ethical approaches, then, will best fit these new leaders?

Two major ethical approaches and principles provide the basis for the leadership: (1) from teleology, the consequentialist approach, which in management is most commonly seen as utilitarianism; and (2) deontology or formalism, which emphasizes duty and which grounds right and wrong in actions themselves (rather than merely consequences) (Christensen, 1988). In the consequentialist utilitarian views, the most good for the most people should prevail (or the least bad, if only bad can occur). In the formalist duty/action view, right actions according to principles apply; e.g., telling the truth, autonomy, acting according to promises. Although an individual may typically hold to one or the other view, it is not unusual to use elements of both positions, depending on the circumstance and time (Andrews and Fargotstein, 1986). Health care workers and managers often favor the consequentialist views (including cost-benefit ratios) when considering the aggregate case, but invoke formalism in the individual case.

In current management, humanism, autonomy, and innovation have become imperative to the establishment of an ethical working environment. Especially in service industries, where caring is as much a product as process, equality and connectedness are suggested to create a more critical ethical climate (Biordi, 1988; Christensen, 1988; Fry, 1988; Moccia, 1988; Reilly, 1989). In light of previous approaches and the newer impetus in management, primary principles that help guide personal conduct and administrative leadership or decision making have been suggested to include autonomy, beneficence, nonmaleficence, justice (Darr, et al., 1986), connectedness, equality, and caring (Biordi, 1988; Christensen, 1988). These principles in turn affect quality of performance, clarity of organizational rules, personal consistency, and integrity, and workers' long-range and short-term perspectives (Morford, 1989).

In humanism and humanistic management, the principle of equality and respect for others gives direction for treating persons as being unique while contributing to the larger community. Autonomy or self-determination is necessary to the promotion of individuals' rights of involvement in decisions that affect their well-being (Christensen, 1988; Darr et al., 1986; McElmurry and Yarling, 1989). For managers, this principle should apply to patients (determining the competency of the patient) and to health care workers, regardless of their position in the hierarchy. These principles are basic to the building of trust, use of confidential information, and daily interactions of etiquette and substance between all types of health care workers and clients.

The concept of beneficence applies especially well to governance structures but can be usefully applied to all workers. Beneficence requires a positive duty to promote good and to avoid harm (Frankena, 1973). This principle can be subdivided into two components: the provision of good (including prevention and/or the removal of harm), and the necessity to balance goods and harms. However, the duty not to inflict harm takes precedence over the promotion of good (Darr et al., 1986; Christensen, 1988).

Similarly, nonmaleficence guides people to refrain from doing harm to others, whether physical or emotional. Beneficence and nonmaleficence are important principles in all areas of organizational life, but they have particular reference in management to fiduciary duty, use of confidential information, and potential conflicts of interest (Chown, 1986; Darr et al., 1986).

Caring and connectedness requires people to actively and explicitly respect the dignity of other human beings and to find ways in which to foster their interdependency without the loss of identity. The primary responsibility of all administrators is to assure the viability of the workgroup (Biordi, 1988). To develop and maintain a workgroup without destroying the essence of the individual members requires that managers develop ways to know and honor their workers' most important values (Fry, 1989). Such knowledge also necessitates a balance between the workers' informed consent and a consideration of the workgroup's long and short term objectives, along with a balance between the beneficence and maleficence of the situation. And most important to the process is the injection of human feeling and emotion.

Although ethicists in the rationalist tradition have tended to regard emotions with skepticism, they are now correctively "rehabilitating" emotions in ethical decision making (S. Callahan, 1988). Emotions now are viewed as a means to energize ethical questioning and invest the ethic with commitment. "Emotional responses, especially moral sentiments, indicate the achievement of self-development and those 'habits of the heart' known as moral character." (S. Callahan, 1988; p. 11). The investment of emotion into ethics recognizes the human characteristic of caring, that is, the feeling of promoting the good of others.

Besides recognizing the importance of character and the good of others, emotions serve as a barometer of moral issues raised by particular disenfranchised groups. Moral revolutions have been initiated or precipitated in the past by slaves, women, workers, children, the handicapped, patients in institutions, and experimental subjects (S. Callahan, 1988). The astute manager will recognize and no longer dismiss the importance of human emotion and caring in all managerial decision making, if only to prevent an otherwise unnecessary revolution. Where pure rationalism once prevailed (a mode of thought widespread in previous management training and extended to nurse managers who hoped to succeed in corporate circles), administrators will now find in "caring" a new tutor and energizer to their ethical reasoning. In the new health care world, nursing administrators and others cannot afford to disregard the subtlety of caring and commitment in the acts and consequences of their management decisions (Dunham, 1989).

As the momentum for caring and commitment takes hold, managers in nursing can facilitate the development of theory in the nature of caring and ethics in two important ways. The first is that nurses, as women and men in a predominantly female profession, particularize an expression of a feminine theory of caring. The nurses' gender and emphasis on caring (both formal and informal caring) can enhance or confound inquiry, depending on the nature of the theoretical question. The second nursing potential goes beyond gender differences in the nature of caring to explore further the notion that "if the ethic of care is a relational ethic, then it is tied to who one is and to what position one occupies in society" (Tronto, 1987, p. 654). Nurse managers, by virtue of their positions as women in a male-dominated society, nurses as a mid-level occupational group and managers in higher positions offer arresting evidence for caring as a duty or a privilege (Reverby, 1987). In terms of moral theory development, the field of nursing and nursing administration offers opportunity to nurses and other theorists who wish to further develop a contextual moral theory of caring.

Equality or justice refers to a fundamental fairness in the treatment of human beings. The question that must be answered is, "What constitutes the legitimate criterion of fairness?" Is fairness (or justice, or equality) to be based on achievement or on merit, greatest need, effort, or contribution? The context often dictates the choice among individual need, effort, contribution, or merit (Aroskar, 1987; Christensen, 1988). However, invocations of context do not easily satisfy those who want a universalist or absolute criterion against which to measure justice. In health care, some writers beg the question of rights to care for all and, using the market model, assert that resources should go most to those who can pay. They argue that this position would then provoke moral candor regarding those who cannot pay for their care and create a more public examination of resource allocation and assumption of costs (Engelhardt and Rie, 1988). For some managers, the allocation of resources and their just stewardship *is* management. How, then, is justice determined best? No more serious question has been put to the American public and health care management.

☐ *Implications for Nursing*

The future will be characterized by constraints: ethicists agree that the microcosms of bioethics committees will face their greatest challenge in maintaining their integrity in the face of cost-containment pressures. Cost-containment will undoubtedly affect the distribution of rare or costly technologies and resources (Medical Ethics Advisor, 1990). Can rationing be far behind?

Ninety-one percent of the Americans believe in the right of all people to have access to the best possible health care. But when the surveys go into details, the numbers begin to drop. Seventy-four percent are willing to have more money spent on care, but, when asked about higher taxation for catastrophic care (estimated to be $125.00 per person) only 1 in 10 were willing to pay higher taxes (D. Callahan, 1988). In the face of the moral dilemma concerning universal care, the American public has opted to avoid the issue, wish for the best, and show no genuine inclination to assume payment for the care. Callahan (1988) argues that it is no accident that serious cost-containment efforts have largely failed. In his view, although most of the public would like to believe in efficiency and the cleverness of technology to address the issues of care distribution, the most rational solution short of bankruptcy is rationing. To even consider this, the most important tasks facing the public and the health care administrator are changing values and searching for the most feasible criterion of justice in care. The public and, indeed, the health care community must soon come to grips with ways to implement "mutual concern, mutual help, mutual sacrifice, and mutual limits" (D. Callahan, 1988). This mutuality of concern and help is the first of the moral imperatives facing health care administrators as leaders in care and caring.

There is a large amount of literature on bioethics, focused primarily on physicians and patients. A second, smaller source of literature is from nursing. These issues and the publishing output of these two professional groups comprise the bulk of the ethics literature, but the focus is frequently particularistic and clinical, close to the patient. Where the literature is less particularized it is enlarged to sweeping concerns of policy. Increasingly, the health care professionals are frustrated, recognizing the limited bipolar focus of views and issues that have occupied the attention of recent ethicists. Somewhere between the protocols of the individual cases and national health care policy are the ethical issues of everyday corporate life. Issues of ethics also apply to other corporate groups and their group relationships of dominance and mutual work support. Yet these issues of group relationships are not addressed (Robbins, 1988; Walker and Norby, 1987, 1988). For example, when the expertise of the physician, nurses, and other co-workers differs regarding treatments or patient care, who should rightfully prevail? And how will the work be organized to create an organizational architecture in which all can more comfortably fit? What legal issues will overlap with the ethical and how? With the movement of care out of hospitals and into homes, what continuity of patient care and patient consent should exist? Who has the responsibility for assuring quality of care, especially when provided in the home by lay persons?

Up to now, it has largely been the physician and the bioethics committees providing the answers. Yet we have seen that nurses, who must implement around-the-clock care, are the least consulted. Major care-providing groups, such as medical records personnel, are privy to confidential information, but except in legal matters this group is almost entirely neglected in the ethics literature. It is imperative that leaders and administrators in the field identify and justly address other relevant groups and their ethical concerns.

Most professional groups have ethical codes. Nurses have one of the most long-standing and clearly written codes of ethics (Viens, 1989). The other non-nursing health care administrators have defined their own codes just within the last decade (Fleck, 1988). With the increasing pressures of high technology, new care, and cost-containment, health care and nursing administrators are functioning within an unprecedented set of constituencies and pressures. Today's health care executive must bargain, sell ideas, and negotiate like a politician (Kanter, 1989). When dealing with so many promises, opportunities, and strategies, executives must have a good memory and solid integrity to continue to steer a steady course. No longer will the issues raised for health care administrators be only those of conflicts of interest (Beall, 1988). Future areas for serious moral inquiry on the part of health care administration in the coming decade will include allegiance to the patient; power; accountability; organizational restructuring; types of motivation (rewards or sanctions); truth in health care advertisement; profitability; health care worker allegiances and alliances with administration; the executive as a moral agent; patient rights; and self, hospital, and community aggrandizement. Some of these suggested areas correspond to those of business and industry, given the impetus of applying principles of retrospective reimbursement and profit maximization to health care.

Health care administrators, however, are in the unique position of not having to repeat the history of business ethics or gaining a similar public perception (only 13% of the American public gave business administrators high or very high ratings) (Business Facts Capsule, 1990). Nursing's code, begun in 1903 and finalized in 1928, stresses caring for the public trust and nurses' commitment to patients. The health care administrators' code, in place since the early 1970s, has been changed to indicate a greater commitment to justice and more realistic processes in responding to complex moral issues (Fleck, 1988). The newer administrative code supports a broader dissemination of a "corporate conscience" that will negate institutional self-interest and sustain the morality endorsed by the code: truthfulness, congruency with other professionals' codes (e.g., ANA, AMA), equitable distribution of resources, colleagueship in a competitive community, and justice in access to care. However, the code reflects the primacy of justice over caring; caring as a precedent is not actively considered at all. This tendency toward justice is in keeping with Kohlberg's (1984) model of moral reasoning, is linked to male gender socialization, and is supported by a variety of other sources when considering medical ethics in general. Therefore, humanistic leaders with vision must find ways to articulate caring with justice, and meaningfully express their vision of caring justice to all health care administrators and staff.

The creative and humanistic nurse administrator will enact and empower others to cultivate a moral discourse that affects the organization as a whole. For it is from the more fully actualized person and in the most empowered group that a full-bodied moral discourse can occur. Power is in the process of being redefined in humanistic management. Previously, power has been defined from any number of bases, but power is ultimately derived from property (including intellectual expertise), the person, and the organization (position and rewards or sanctions) (Moore, 1988).

Although position power is often thought to be the most lasting, executives are counseled to shape their personality power and interpersonal and work skills, since those are transportable from one site to another. In light of these admonitions, we can consider Janet Hagberg's (1984) description of power, which she relates to stages of personal growth. Hagberg's (1984) stages are analogous to those suggested in Kohlberg's (1984) model of moral development. Her first three stages of power are externally oriented: powerlessness, power by association, and power by symbols. The remaining three stages are internally oriented: power by reflection (modeling integrity and inspiring hope), power by purpose (empowering others, inspiring love, and service), and power by gestalt (leading others and inspiring inner peace). In the last stage she states that power of the morally mature person is universalistic in its development of the unity of inner peace and its inspiration to others.

Such an elegant unity of individual morality and power explains inspirational moral leadership and its link to the organization. The conventional wisdom of nursing administrators and popularists regarding the necessity for moral integrity has its theoretical correspondence in the individual and moves the apprehension of ethics beyond the individual to the organization.

Making ethics a serious part of the administrative domain and developing the inquiry beyond the micropolitical level of patient-related decision making is, and will continue to be, the major social responsibility of the practicing administrator. The conduct of such inquiry requires that administration and staff alike collaborate to develop a work environment that has as its most basic approach a genuine respect and caring for people. People are, after all, the most important assets of any organization. Ethical awareness and sensitivity to others requires constant practice and reflection – in short, strategizing and commitment. Thus, to solve a moral problem, the nurse leader must consider and link (1) a changing view of the facts (which are not necessarily immutable); (2) a change in feelings; and (3) a change in action (Midgley, 1987).

Strategies to enhance a principled reasoning process must be based in a nursing leader's clear view of the major ethical approaches and their derived principles. In managing the moral issues, and following many of Christensen's suggestions (1988), the following steps would be useful to the nurse leader of the future. First, the nature of the problem should be examined for its essential issue and subsequent moral concern, including the nature of the moral agent, the values and data invoked, and its relevancy to other areas of the organization or people. (This may require a comparison of the professional codes of ethics of all professionals and administrators involved.) Second, the relevant viewpoints and data of all individuals involved in the situation should be sought and developed in regard to an action plan. Third, the basic approaches and ethical principles must be applied to the identified issue and action to determine their moral coherency and defensibility. Fourth, the nurse administrator must make, enact, and evaluate a particular choice; otherwise, inactivated choices fall more in the realm of attitudes than of actions.

For the nurse executives and other health care administrators of the 1990s, the major moral issues that emerge essentially relate to the injection of caring into the organizational enterprise; the allocation of scarce health care resources; limitations; confidentiality and privacy; and how all of these are managed at the organizational and national levels. Professional expertise is only partially prepared for the moral task: administrators, patients, and communities are seeing the need to become more active in their participation in moral decision making. Relationships among all of these groups will change, and therefore power and expertise will be questioned and monitored using new and tighter controls. Ethics committees, which now exist in 60% of the institutions surveyed (Edwards and Haddad, 1988) reduce moral risk, but their own integrity is being threatened by cost constraints. Rationing, euthanasia, technological advances, and treatment plans will likely be politicized as well as moralized. Principles of caring, autonomy, justice, beneficence, and nonmaleficence will be applied by the morally concerned to problems never before imagined. Administrators will be called upon to take leadership in more humane, creative ways at a time when fewer workers will be available in the economy. The future is challenging. But nursing administrators, ever the wise partners, can help restructure health care if they take to heart the elements of moral reasoning and execute their rightful place in doing good.

☐ Application to Nursing: Case Study

A staff nurse, Joan, who worked on a psychiatric unit at Elsewhere General, was suspected of diverting drugs for her personal use (addiction). Joan was also suspected of obtaining drugs to give them to her boyfriend, who then sold them. After obtaining this report from the head nurse of the psychiatric unit, the nursing associate director (in charge of psychiatric, medical, and obstetrical nursing) ordered the head nurse to obtain additional evidence before taking action. The head nurse approached a second staff nurse, Suzanne, who was known to be a friend of Joan's and requested Suzanne's assistance in getting Joan to therapy and off drugs.

Suzanne was asked to speak to Joan and, if she verified that Joan was taking the narcotics, to suggest that Joan would benefit from therapy. However, since narcotic-diversions were grounds for dismissal in that organization, Suzanne was assured by the head nurse that Joan would not lose her job if she acknowledged taking the drugs and that the organization would make every effort to facilitate Joan's rehabilitation. As a concerned friend, Suzanne agreed to speak to Joan.

Joan acknowledged her addiction and the diversion of drugs. She denied giving any to her boyfriend. Joan asked Suzanne to act as an intermediary and to accompany her as she spoke to the head nurse when she reported her diversion. Both nurses made an appointment to speak to the head nurse.

When they arrived at the appointment, the head nurse was there with her associate director. This surprised Suzanne and Joan, who had not expected to see both administrators and had not been informed about the appearance of the associate director. Nevertheless, Joan proceeded to report her diversion. After Joan spoke, the associate director informed her that she would be subject to dismissal. Shortly thereafter, Joan was dismissed. The administrators did not discuss matters further with Suzanne. Suzanne, feeling betrayed by the administrators, went to the vice president of nursing and reported her bitterness, outrage, and sense of betrayal.

Questions for Discussion

1. Taking into account the ethical principles cited in this chapter, and placing yourself in the position of the vice president of nursing, what might your response be to Suzanne? Now, imagine yourself speaking to Suzanne only as a personal friend. Would your response be different, and in what way? Be sure to cite each principle, or any other rationale you use, and their relationship to this case.

2. Again, taking into account this chapter's views, how else do you think the head nurse could have proceeded in discovering more fully the facts of Joan's diversions? What other positions do you think Suzanne could have taken in response to her head nurse's request? Support your position, using points taken from this chapter.

3. If you were an administrator, how do you think you would handle *several* cases of drug diversion in this same agency? Does an aggregation make a difference in your moral response?

4. In your nursing practice or personal life, can you say which of the ethical systems discussed in this chapter best reflect your choices? Do you find

differences in the ethical criteria by which you judge personal and practice events? What are these, and how do you reconcile any differences (if they exist)?

5. As a woman, have you ever been told that you think like a man? Was this statement meant to be flattering? Or, as a man, have you ever been told that you think like a woman? Was this statement meant to be flattering? Given your gender, what do you think would be the implications for you if you were to reexamine and perhaps change your ethical systems? What would happen to your friendships; work relationships; significant other or spousal relationships?

6. Given the recent concerns about resource reallocation in health care, what is your opinion of rationing of health care? For premature infants? For elders? For people in your family? Use principles in this chapter to help formulate your views.

References

Andrews, M., and Fargotstein, B. (1986). International nursing consultation: a perspective on ethical issues. *Journal of Professional Nursing, 2*(5), 302-308.

Aroskar, M. (1987). The interface of ethics and politics in nursing. *Nursing Outlook, 35*(6), 268-271.

Beall, J. (1988). Examining corporate conscience: An exercise for quality assurance. *Health Progress, 69*(9), 24-25.

Bennis, W. (1989). *On becoming a leader.* Menlo Park, Calif.: Addison Wesley Publishing.

Biordi, D. (1986). Nursing service administrators: marginality and the public person. *Nursing Clinics of North America, 21*(1), 173-183.

Biordi, D. (April, 1988). Nursing Administrators: The nature of their work and error identification. Paper presented at the 12th annual meeting of the Midwest Nursing Research Society, Wichita, Kan.

Business Facts Capsule. (1990, Jan). *Chicago Tribune*

Callahan, D. (1988). Allocating health resources. *Hastings Center Report. 18*(2), 14-20.

Callahan, S. (1988). The role of emotion in ethical decision making. *Hastings Center Report, 18*(3), 9-14.

Chown, E. (1986). Ethical decisions: no simple recipe. *Hospital Trustee, 10*(1), 4-5.

Christensen, P. (1988). An ethical framework for nursing service administration. *Advances in Nursing Science, 10*(3), 46-55.

Curtin, L., and Flaherty, M. J. (1982). *Nursing Ethics: Theories and Pragmatics.* Bowie, Md.: Robert J. Brady, Co.

Daley-Gawenda, D., Feldman, J., and Biordi, D. (1986). Retrenchment: weathering the crisis. *Nursing Management, 17*(8), 20-26.

Darr, K., Longest, B., and Rakich, J. (1986). The ethical imperative in health services governance and management. *Hospital and Health Services Administration, 31*(2), 53-66.

Drucker, P. (1966). *The effective executive.* New York: Harper & Row, p. 52.

Dunham, J. (1989). The art of humanistic nursing administration: expanding the horizons. *Nursing Administrative Quarterly, 13*(3), 55-66.

Edwards, B., and Haddad, A.M. (1988). Establishing a nursing bioethics committee. *Journal of Nursing Administration, 18*(3), 30-33.

Engelhardt, H., and Rie, M. (1988). Morality for the medical-industrial complex. A code of ethics for the mass marketing of health care. *The New England Journal of Medicine, 319*(16), 1088-1089.

Fleck, L. (1988). Evaluating executive ethics: Is the ACHE code enough? *Michigan Hospital, 24*(12), 13-18.

Frankena, W. (1973). *Ethics,* ed 2, Englewood Cliffs, N.J.: Prentice Hall.

Fry, S. (1988). The ethic of caring: can it survive in nursing? *Nursing Outlook, 36*(1), 48.

Fry, S. (1989). The ethics of compromise. *Nursing Outlook, 37*(3), 152.

Garner, R., and Rosen, B. (1967). *Moral Reasoning.* New York: Macmillan.

Gilligan, C. (1982). *In a different voice.* Cambridge, Mass.: Harvard University Press.

Grier, D. (1989). Confronting ethical dilemmas. The view from inside—a practitioner's perspective. Presentation to the Canadian Centre for Ethics and Corporate Policy, Toronto, Sept. 19, 1989.

Hagberg, J. (1984). *Real power: the stages of personal power in organizations.* Minneapolis: The Winston Press.

Jackall, R., (1988). *Moral mazes: The world of corporate managers.* New York: Oxford University Press.

Jameton, A. (1984). *Nursing practice: the ethical issues.* Englewood Cliffs, N.J.: Prentice Hall.

Jones, R.: Personal communication, May 1989.

Kanter, P. (1989). The new managerial work. *Harvard Business Review, 67*(6), 85-92.

Kohlberg, L. (1984). Essays on moral development: the psychology of moral development. New York: Harper & Row.

McCall, M.W., and Lombardo, M.M. (1983). What makes a top executive? *Psychology Today, 17*(2), 30-32.

McElmurry, B., and Yarling, E. (1989). Guest editorial. *Advances in Nursing Science, 11*(3), xi.

MacPherson, K. (1989). A new perspective on nursing and caring in a corporate context. *Advances in Nursing Science, 11*(4), 32-39.

Medical Ethics Advisor. (1990). Experts: cost will shape bioethics in the 1990s. *Medical Ethics Advisor, 6*(1), 1-16.

Midgley, M. (1987). The flight from blame. *Philosophy, 62,* 271-291.

Moccia, P. (1988). At the faultline: Social activism and caring. *Nursing Outlook, 36*(1), 30-33.

Moore, T. (1988). The ethics of power. *Michigan Hospital, 24*(12), 7-12.

Morford, J. (1989). Values and leadership: ten basic rules. *Topics in Health Record Management, 9*(3), 1-6.

Noddings, N. (1984). *Caring: A feminine approach to ethics and moral education.* Berkeley: University of California Press.

Omery, A. (1989). Values, moral reasoning, and ethics. *Nursing Clinics of North America, 24*(2), 499-508.

Reilly, D. (1989). Ethics and values in nursing: are we opening Pandora's box? *Nursing & Health Care, 2,* 91-95.

Reverby, S.M. (1987). *Ordered to care.* New York: Cambridge University Press.

Robbins, D. (1988). Toward integrated clinical/administrative ethics policies in health care. *Michigan Hospitals, 24*(12), 19-22.

Schrock, R. (1980). A question of honesty in nursing practice. *Journal of Advanced Nursing, 5,* 135-148.

Singer, M. (1961, reprinted 1971). *Generalization in ethics.* New York: A. Knopf.

Theis, E. (1986). Ethical issues. A nursing perspective. *The New England Journal of Medicine, 315*(19), 1222-1224.

Tronto, J.C. (1987). Beyond gender difference to a theory of care. *Signs: Journal of women in culture and society, 12*(4), 644-663.

Viens, D. (1989). A history of nursing's code of ethics. *Nursing Outlook, 37*(1), 45-49.

Walker, M., and Norby, R. (1987, 1988). Friendships of utility: Resolving the disalignment between nursing education and nursing service. *Nursing Forum, 23*(1), 30-35.

Yarling, R., and McElmurry, B. (1986). The moral foundation of nursing. *Advances in Nursing Science, 8*(2), 63-73.

Young, L.C., and Hayne, A.N. (1988). *Nursing Administration: From Concepts to Practice.* Philadelphia: W.B. Saunders Company.

5

JUDE A. MAGERS

Creating Culture

CHAPTER OBJECTIVES

☐ Describe the impact of external forces that are
influencing cultural change within the health
care field.

☐ Explain the need to articulate values and
beliefs that are foundations in clinical
practice.

☐ Identify three skills required in cultural
leadership.

Health care organizations in the United States are continuing to evolve through individual life cycles as external and internal realities compel systems to change. "Health care organizations and hospitals in particular are under siege, and the industry is responding with a host of new strategies such as downsizing, cost reduction, vigorous marketing efforts, and vertical integration" (Kaluzney, 1989, p. 40). Management skills are focusing on productivity, standard measurements, information management systems, and financial cost analysis. The world of health care executives from lower management through corporate executive officers has radically changed in the last 30 years. Administrators in the 1960s were usually registered nurses and social service oriented professionals whose primary purposes were caring, compassion, and assuring delivery of human services. Health care services were discussed as "patient centered," available to any person suffering from trauma, acute physical illness, or chronic mental illness. The delivery systems were structured to express the values of a safe, caring, and curative nature. Health care givers were oriented to provide "state of the art" services to anyone who came through the door of the clinic, emergency room, or admitting office. If there were problems with a hospital or clinic's admission criteria, an ill person could travel to a nearby health care system and receive a comparable level of services.

Inflationary factors in the U.S. economy during the 1970s and early 1980s brought acute attention to the Gross National Product and the resources attributed to the health care system. In the 1980s, basic assumptions of access and utilization of health care services were challenged, changed, and redefined. These changes resulted from the focus on the national debt, growing international markets, rising costs of medical technology, high expenses in medical research and development, extension of life expectancies, and the increased need of services for the chronically ill. Rapid changes began to occur to revamp policies about how to pay for services and to be more fiscally responsible. Cost containment affected all aspects of health care delivery.

The 1990s opened upon a changed, evolving culture in the health care arena. Basic assumptions are in flux. Emerging patterns include changes in availability levels; access based on ability to pay; rationing of services; increased outpatient services for high acuity care needs; and increasing external regulations designed by providers of reimbursement. In the midst of these dramatic changes, the public demands quality health care services: state of the art, positive outcomes; caring and compassion; access to services; availability without debt; and the right to information. Health care executives who once enjoyed strong internal control of their organizations now must fashion health care to be responsive to strong external pressures. The health care culture of the last century has evolved from a social response system to a business. The health care executive, acting responsibly amid current realities, must manage for financial success and show leadership geared toward effectiveness and quality results.

Fiscal responsibility and positive outcomes alone will not meet the expectations of all consumers. It is in leadership that a desirable and integral health care system will be achieved, exhibiting success in the 1990s. Leadership in the 1990s must help to make sense of the changes that occurred in the 1980s. Health care executives at all levels need to create a new and viable health care culture. Cultural leadership is a necessity. Cultural leadership must help the health care team—professionals, paraprofessionals, and support staff—to understand the impact of the 1980s on delivery of services. Dissonance resulting from staff assumptions regarding quality practice versus cost containment measures by administration adds tension, conflict, and dysfunction within a health care system unless efforts are made to clarify and redefine the culture of the organization.

Cultural Awareness

Wilkins (1983 p. 25) provides insight into five conditions that prompt cultural awareness: (1) diversification, (2) adaptation of competitive strategy, (3) rapid growth, (4) serious conflict between groups in organizations, and (5) reductions within organizations. These situations have been at the heart of health care organizational change. These realities change the culture of an organization.

In leadership literature, Peters and Waterman (1982), Bennis and Nanus (1985), Clemens and Mayer (1987), and Zaleznik (1989) addressed components of culture: mission, vision making, value oriented behavior, ownership, participation, shared meaning, incentives, rewards, and image.

In *Leadership,* Burns (1979) presented a comprehensive discussion emphasizing the interaction between leaders and followers and the importance of everyday leadership effectiveness and motivating followers. The health care executive who understands cultural leadership and its vital importance for success works to mobilize health care practitioners to define today's assumptions, articulate values, and structure effective quality delivery systems. If the executive focuses only on fiscal soundness in the traditional bureaucratic structures of health care, the outcome will be failure and the death of the organization. Leadership as creating culture is based on the principles of transformational leadership. "The transforming leader looks for potential motives in followers, seeks to satisfy higher needs, and engages the full person of the follower" (Burns, 1979, p. 4). Today's executive cannot act alone in an ivory tower but must use the dynamic energy of the membership to create a successful, sense-making health care culture.

Sense Making

"Retrospective explanations are produced through a particular thinking process that [is called] sense making" (Louis, 1980, p. 240). Louis (1980) proposed that when individuals work, much of the "how to do" and "what to do" operate at an unconscious level. It is when the unusual occurs that the person must consciously problem-solve to understand, make sense of the world, and cope with instability, change, and the unexpected. This sense-making process must occur between leadership and followership for successful outcomes. Sense making assists members to articulate effective experiences from the past, actively participate in change to experience internal control, recognize shared meaning among other members, and utilize personal traits and characteristics (Louis, 1980, p. 241).

Organizational membership in health care must consciously restructure the workplace to make sense of overlapping values rooted in personal, societal, professional, and corporate histories. This conscious sense-making activity is the key activity in creating culture. Cultural leadership remains sensitive to the ambiguity caused by the initial sense-making process and the outcome of creating culture. To help control ambiguity, leadership carries out the critical role of vision setter. The leadership helps the followership to see where it is going while the present feels uncertain and conflictive. The cultural leader remains involved in continued evaluation of the effectiveness of the organization.

Life Cycle

The health care executive needs to assess the position of the organization within its traditional life cycle and determine strategies to define a culture that is adaptive to constant change. Understanding life cycle phases in health care is critical because an organization can easily die in today's business environment. The cultural leader in health care no longer can be satisfied with maintenance and "doing it the way we have always done it."

Cameron and Whetton (1983) conducted a review of life cycle models identified in a variety of organizations. Common to all the models are four stages: entrepreneurial, collectivity, formalization and control, and elaboration of structure (pp. 282, 283). The health care executive must restructure the organization to be adaptable to these four stages. Traditional bureaucracy of health care systems, characterized by the formalization and control stage, can halt growth and keep the system unable to adapt to necessary change. At the same time, the health care staff may want to remain in the safe and predictable patterns of formalization and control. Herein lies the work of the cultural leader: to keep the membership of the organizational structure adaptive to a dynamic life cycle.

Matrix management was a common response to the dilemma of bureaucratic structures in the 1980s. It required transition to diversification, decentralization, and vertical integration. The health care leader who facilitated transition into the matrix structure and product line management had as an undesirable common outcome an undesirable ambiguity in purpose, roles and "expected behavior" (Meyer and Merrell, 1984, p. 36). External forces have simultaneously demanded change within the health care organization and created additional ambiguity. Ambiguity created by healthy and necessary transition through the organizational life cycle requires the skills of cultural leadership.

Cultural Leadership

Cultural leadership is played out in human interactions and patterns of basic assumptions expressed through values, rituals, symbols, and rites of passage. Values are at the core of the organization's culture. Values are the structural components that support the product of the organization. Health care values have traditionally been quality, state-of-the-art technology, trustworthiness, caring, and accessibility to the public. The 1990s speak of quality and cost containment, collaborative relations between payors, health care providers, physicians, and the industry.

Rituals "are the systematic and programmed routines of day to day life in the company" (Deal and Kennedy, 1982, p. 14). "Strong culture companies go to the trouble of spelling out, often in copious detail, the routine behavioral rituals they expect their employees to follow" (Deal and Kennedy, 1982, p. 14). Rites of passage are formal rituals that are corporately or departmentally defined to explicitly state values of the organization. Rituals in health care can be seen among patients' routines: wearing a gown; being confined to a room; eating at specific times; and being identified by a room number or by diagnosis. Rituals for professionals include wearing white lab coats, white caps, stethoscopes, and responding to patients by answering a "call light." Examples of rites of passage include attaining seniority, certification permitting advancement, career ladders, retirement celebrations, and restructuring to promote equity across job classifications.

Symbols conveying explicit health care messages can be seen across landscapes as light beacons, crosses, and highway signs (a white "H" on a blue background). Rituals, rites of passage, and symbols are undergoing transitions characterized by fewer people answering call lights, early retirement, and conditional access to many hospitals.

Health care industries continue to identify values, rituals, and rites of passage within the cultural boundaries of delivery systems. The cultural leader defines cultural boundaries by the process of "differential interaction" (Maanen and Barley, 1985, p. 34). Differential interaction is the group member's internal networking as contrasted with communication outside the group. Differential interaction can lead to "collective understandings" that are essential to cultural expression (Maanen and Barley, 1985, p. 35). There are deeply rooted collective understandings such as vertical dominated decision making, top level control, rigid interpretation of policy, and the "we-they" relationship between administration and clinical staff. These understandings are formed within the bureaucratic phase of the health care organization's life cycle. The radical movement to the stage of "elaboration of structure" (Cameron and Whetton, 1983) commonly seen in fiscally successful health care systems in the 1980s has met with confusion among membership as collective understandings changed. Health care systems designed "products" for the market that represented mixed results: high revenue, low mission; high revenue, high mission; low revenue, low mission; and high mission, low revenue. Traditional health care membership, accustomed to working day-to-day on assumptions supporting high mission for patient care, suddenly felt alienated in a new professional practice setting that still resembled the old in many ways. Cultural leadership became acutely necessary to its membership to rearticulate its collective understandings through redesigning its rites, rituals, and symbols. A new culture in health care began to emerge in the 1980s.

Deal and Kennedy (1982, p. 14) refer to rites and rituals as mechanisms to express expected behavior in the culture. Pettigrew (1979, p. 575) emphasizes the role of language in creating culture, integrating behavior, and motivating to action. Smircich (1983, p. 347) comments that culture expressed through symbolism is a manifestation of human consciousness. Cultural leadership demonstrated by health care executives at all levels of management uses the rituals, rites of passage, and symbols of its membership to decrease ambiguity and increase sense making and shared meaning between the goals and expectations of the organization and its individual membership. This shared meaning is critical in understanding "why it is done," "what is done," and "how it is done." Kilmann (1989, p. 49-50) states, "Every organization has an invisible quality – a certain style, a character, a way of doing things – that ultimately determines whether success will be achieved. Culture is the invisible force behind the tangibles and observables in an organization, a social energy that moves the people into action."

Kilmann (1989, p. 51) suggests that to manage culture successfully it is imperative to know how cultures form and continue to remain intact. Kilmann

(1989) proposes five steps for assuring successful management of culture, as shown in Figure 5-1.

Schein (1985, p. 9), in his definition of culture, adds an important dimension to the management of culture:

> ". . . a pattern of basic assumptions invented, discovered, or developed by a given group as it learns to cope with its problems of external adaptation and internal integration—that has worked well enough to be considered valid and, therefore, to be taught to new members as the correct way to perceive, think, and feel in relation to those problems."

Schein (1985) suggests that culture is carried on by the individual and can be learned. Because it is deeply embedded, patterned behavior, its expression by rituals, rites of passage, and symbols, is something to which the cultural leader must be sensitive. As the new business of health care in the United States defines its culture by keeping valid assumptions, revising old beliefs, or articulating new values, the health care executive's cultural leadership skills must reevaluate traditional symbolic behavior. Do the old ways of doing things continue to be effective in today's culture? Leadership must reassess all aspects of its corporate

Steps:	Method:
1. Surface actual norms	Group membership articulates norms believed to be in place (without superiors present).
2. Establish desired norms	Group membership articulates desired norms (without superiors present).
3. Identify culture gaps	Administer Kilmann-Saxton Culture Gap Survey* and review with membership.
4. Close culture gaps	Build desired norms into a sanctioning system, e.g., appraisal system, unit specific structure, quality control mechanism.
5. Sustaining culture changes	Continue evaluation. Repeat Kilmann-Saxton Survey 6 to 9 months.

Fig. 5-1 .Steps for managing culture. Modified from Kilmann R.H., *Managing beyond the quick fix.,*
*Kilmann, R.H., Saxton, M.J.: The Kilmann-Saxton Culture-Gap Survey, Pittsburgh, 1983: Organizational Design Consultants. Distributed by Xicom, Inc., Sterling Forest Tuxedo, NY 10987. (800)759-4266.

system: definition of mission, statement of philosophy, strategic planning in a vertically integrated system, personnel policies, reward and incentive plans for goals that address mission and revenue, marketing strategy to specific target groups rather than everyone, and image-making for credibility among all consumers.

Rituals that once supported access to health care by physician's orders are now subject to preauthorization by the payor, ability to pay, and selective diagnosis. Rituals that once required the professional practitioner are now replaced by high technology and less skilled employees. Rites of passage that used to encourage advancement and retention are now subject to cost containment measures. The use of language as organizational symbols demonstrates a financial basis instead of a quality mission for health care.

Cultural leadership in the health care organization recognizes the power of culture and the need to manage culture proactively, and it respects the integrity of the desired culture by its membership. Culture is not known by isolating decision making, vision setting, and strategic planning from a leader's followership. Culture is discovered, nurtured, and refined in the interaction of cultural leadership and followership. Nanus (1989, p. 51) states, "Empowerment works because it supports the deepest psychological needs of followers." Thus, cultural leadership must ensure congruity between decision making practices and strategic planning. Followers need effectiveness in professional practice, ownership in the work setting, a trusting environment, a sense of security, adequate recognition, rewards, and meaningful work.

Bennis and Nanus (1985, p. 85) refer to four strategies for effective leadership. These strategies are relevant to the skills of cultural leadership: (1) the clarity of vision that results in commitment of followership, (2) the development of shared meaning, (3) the positioning of the culture to adapt to ambiguous and external ecological forces, and (4) the ability of the leadership to remain open and collaborative with the membership so that the organization learns and develops through its life cycle. The skills of cultural leadership facilitate the development of a strong culture, help the culture adapt to change, and support membership in times of ambiguity and departure from "old ways of doing things." Cultural leadership is the emerging vista in health care organizations. Cultural leadership is not new but is desperately needed as a new culture emerges.

The cultural leader must utilize a central skill identified by Schein (1985, p. 16) as "cognitive transformation." In cognitive transformation, the belief that there is a valued way of problem solving is moved from a group's conscious level of expression or behavior to its unconscious level. The cultural leader in today's health care system must facilitate cognitive transformation in the areas of (1) accessing health care, (2) making adequate health care available, (3) rationing care, (4) measuring competency in providing care, (5) providing cost effective care, and (6) providing necessary services.

This demand for cultural leadership requires participative decision making, shared governance models, collaborative practice models, and excellence in practice—all within limited resources. Basic assumptions and beliefs that are generated and validated by this process create the new culture. As success continues, the health care group keeps the desired rituals, rites, and symbols. The group becomes empowered as it participates in determining what works and what can be retained to pass on to new members.

The health care organizational culture must retain quality patient/family care as a central core assumption to retain credibility among consumers (Figure 5-2). Quality patient/family care is achieved by cultural leadership through three steps: (1) continual vision setting, (2) continual sense making with internal and external relationships to the system, and (3) cognitive transformation. Figure 5-2 depicts the continuous movement of culture development within the context of the environment. Membership within the health care organization actively participates in explicitly stating the mission and philosophy of the system. In the transition from traditional health care to the emerging health care culture, Kilmann's (1989) model for cultural formation is suggested as a viable means to surface assumptions and beliefs. Assumptions and beliefs are reference points for stating mission and philosophy. Cultural leaders utilize the mission and philosophy to ground their visions for successful health care services and make frequent explicit references to both mission and philosophy. Mission and philosophy act as dynamic forces within the sense-making processes led by cultural leadership.

Sense making helps the membership check with each other for what has worked, what seems not to work, and what new ways can be tried to respond to internal beliefs in the corporate mission and philosophy. Figure 5-2 supports active participation necessary for sense making. Active participation requires critical principles of integrity/trust, motivation to excellence, interdependency/collaboration, and ownership/stewardship. Active participative principles vary in intensity and have elasticity based upon the life cycle stage of the organization. The culture of the organization is developed from the strengths of the active participative principles. A strong culture in a health care organization demonstrates clear behavior in communication, creativity, leadership, and teamwork, as well as clear concepts of compassion and human dignity.

Behaviors can be identified by rituals, rites of passage, and symbols (language or action). When the behaviors are unclear, ambiguous, or inconsistent, the active participative principles tend to be weak. Weakness results from the lack of cultural leadership, organizational life cycle transition, or overpowering external ecological forces. Standards of practice influenced by advancing knowledge, technology, and/or regulatory agencies and exacerbated by the economic reality of limited resources continuously affects cultural development.

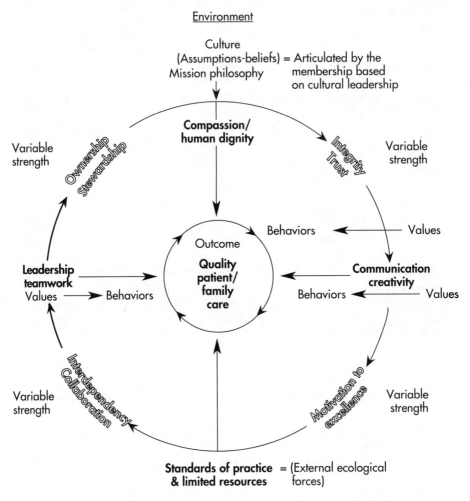

Fig. 5-2. Conceptual framework for health care systems based on life cycle stage of organization. Copyright 1990 by J.A. Magers. By permission of J.A. Magers.

The experiences of successful corporations outside of health care verify the positive results of cultural leadership (Peters and Waterman, 1982; Deal and Kennedy, 1982; Nanus, 1989). Research in the area of organizational culture and effectiveness (Denison and Mishra, 1989) provides empirical evidence that components of culture affect desired outcomes. Denison and Mishra (1989, p. 168-69) present four common hypotheses for organizational effectiveness:

1. Involvement and participation by membership promote ownership and stewardship,
2. Consistency in shared meaning (beliefs, values, symbols) that are understood by membership can lead to organizational effectiveness,
3. Adaptability, or the membership's ability to use learned ways of doing things or change to learn new ways that work, and
4. Mission that provides meaning, which in turn leads membership to structure effective behavior congruent with the mission of the organization.

The empirical results of this research are very encouraging and support all four hypotheses, particularly mission and involvement (Denison and Mishra, p. 172).

Harris (1989) developed a research design to consider a model of culture and mapping processes. The model supports the work of individuals to create culture as they interpret experiences and define their behaviors (Figure 5-3).

The presentation by Harris supports the perspective that "organizational culture is a patterned system of shared, individual-level, organizational-specific schemes" (Harris, 1989, p. 178). The study also emphasizes the power of the formalized leader in the creation of culture. Harris (1989, p. 180) states

> The model . . . provides a framework that (1) highlights the relative power of the agents in the organization who control the nature of the objective environment, (2) emphasizes the importance of symbolic and non-symbolic activity in shaping organizational reality (the dashed arrows), and (3) clarifies the process by which organizational cultures can be changed.

The cultural leader directs and functions within a course of planned change. Kilmann (1989) provides a framework for planned change. He emphasizes that success depends upon the need to identify the complexity of variables—obstacles and opportunities; to take inventory of possible mechanisms to control variables; and to specify ongoing activities that manage the desired settings for change.

Kilmann (1989) places the mechanisms to control the critical variables for successful change into five tracks: culture, management skills, team building, strategy-structure, and reward system. The tracks are capable of facilitating change within the environment and aggregate group as well as at the individual level. The implementation of the tracks is dynamic, complex, and flexible. Each track has a specific intent in its application. The culture track is aimed at adaptation to expected behaviors characterized by trust, flexibility, and openness. Management skills development focuses on problem identification, evaluation, and positive outcomes. Team building is the catalyst to operationalize the culture and management skill tracks. Strategy-structure is an integration of mission, philosophy, and vision for organizational success with the concerns of the team

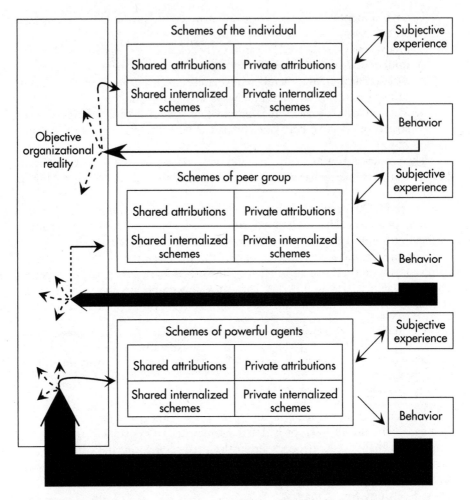

Fig. 5-3. Model of culture and scheme dynamics. By permission of S.G. Harris, Auburn University. Conceptualized by S.G. Harris, A schema-based perspective on organizational culture, Auburn University, Department of Management, Auburn, Ala.

members: Where are we going? What is in it for me? and, How will we get to our future? Without the first three tracks, strategy-structure cannot be expected to achieve its goal: providing working structures to achieve desired outcomes. The fifth track is the reward system. The reward track sets in place the channels for extrinsic rewards for the organization's members. As organizational success is realized, the membership is overtly recognized for directly influencing the desired successful outcomes.

☐ *Implications for Nursing*

The transformational changes occurring in American health care systems will continue throughout the 1990s. Some systems will not survive because they will not be able to finance operations or, more importantly, will not be able to change their corporate cultures to respond to internal and external assumptions. Curtin (1989) comments on the continued struggle of hospitals and health care professionals in taking on the characteristics of business. The basic assumption that health care in the United States is a "right" is being questioned, and a new culture is on the horizon.

If administrators are to show cultural leadership, they must interact with members at all levels of the organization. The health care giver must be able to communicate present work-setting symbols, rituals, and rites of passage. Leadership, to be considered cultural leadership, must have an intuitive sense and listen attentively to the storytelling of its followership: its symbolic language, references to rituals, and themes in behavior. Common daily routines need to be evaluated not only for management productivity outcomes, but also for cultural leadership design and creation of new viable visions. To change a ritual without respecting its foundation of assumptions is to cause confusion, dissatisfaction, apathy, and loss of desire to perform. As cultural leadership unravels the connection between belief and behavior in the health care organization, a new and desired vision can be articulated, controlling the ambiguity of radical changes and encouraging integrity for the health care provider. The outcome is culture.

"A strong, cohesive culture promotes good performance and high job satisfaction. When organizations find ways of articulating shared values, norms, and beliefs, employees are guided in similar directions" (Calhoun, 1989, p. 112). Cultural leadership facilitates the creation of culture.

☐ *Application to Nursing: Case Study*

The director of nursing of a 120-bed mental health inpatient program located in the Midwest used the framework of cultural leadership to facilitate behavioral and structural change within the organization. The impetus for change was based on significant external factors and internal reaction to the stress of the health care environment. The mental health delivery system had witnessed a 40% decrease in length of stay (LOS) in less than two years, continued restrictions in Medicare reimbursement, a 50% increase in managed care capitation at an average of 30% below actual cost, and decreasing admissions due to changing LOS. The labor market was an additional external factor putting stress on the ability to hire professional staff at competitive salaries while maintaining internal labor expenses within a decreasing budget.

The director of nursing, working within the traditional structure of the management team, discussed the need for change in the "way we have always done things." Formal and informal communications, round table discussions, and strategic planning meetings were used as channels for initiating the process of cognitive transformation among the key management personnel of the facility. This process highlighted the reality of a changing environment and the "obvious" need for change in day-to-day practices. Management staff agreed that they consistently experienced increased stress, feelings of getting further behind, decreasing support for completing tasks, and vague feelings of loss of control in their assigned areas of responsibility. The management staff identified the need for change and supported the possibility that the system could restructure to accommodate the rapid changes occurring around them. The director facilitated a vision for successful outcomes by describing a shared governance framework with a 3-year time line for implementing a basic structure and by providing input to management from external experts in the field of shared governance. The director and management staff then began to network with clinical staff formally and informally to determine the clinicians' perceptions of their adequacy and the appropriateness of their clinical practice. Within a 3-month period of assessment, the impressions and data they gathered validated the need for cultural change. The clinicians stated that (1) they had less time to complete work; (2) they were tired of duplication; (3) their interventions had minimal outcome due to decreasing LOS; (4) they had less tolerance of perceived incompetence; and (5) they had no opportunity to exchange valuable information with team members. The clinicians perceived that what they valued in their practice they could no longer express or conduct. A critical warning given by the staff was that quality was being lost.

The assessment of the perceptions by the clinicians was supported by a pilot survey of the lead RNs from each program and each shift. The Kilmann-Saxton Culture-Gap Survey was administered to 25 registered nurses in leadership roles. In general the findings showed significant gaps in the staff's ability to initiate change, to carry on satisfying social interaction in the work environment, and to claim ownership in outcomes of the work setting. These perceptions suggested a negative affect on patient outcome.

The management staff discussed principles of shared governance among the clinicians. There were initial feelings of fear, uncertainty, resistance, and confusion. The ambiguity was to be expected as part of the cultural change and was explained to staff as being necessary for restructuring the organization. The clinicians were invited over a 6-month period to a variety of planned programs on shared governance. Following 6 months of preparation among the management and clinicians, the director set forth a 5-year developmental plan for restructuring the culture for shared governance. The values and beliefs desired by the clinicians were built into the model for shared governance. The clinicians received the plan openly and recognized that this was a viable avenue to change practice patterns so they would fit the present-day stresses. The clinicians did not deny the challenges ahead, yet they were ready for change and the opportunity to determine their future. This preparation time to change the culture took 18 months.

The professional staff initially worked directly with management to revise policies and procedures, job descriptions, and personnel performance tools. The traditional structure needed to be changed in language and rituals (procedures) to reflect principles of shared governance. Critical in this process was the ability of management and staff to articulate values and beliefs of professional practice. Key staff within patient program areas formed educational and process groups to gain self-insights into group dynamics, decision making models, negotiation skills, and personal strengths. Shared governance principles were integrated into any process that involved structural or behavioral changes.

The next 5 years will position the structure within a new culture of shared governance. Staff from across management and clinical lines will be helped to be interactive, collaborative, and accountable for their practice in delivering quality patient and family care. The shared governance structures will define new rituals, symbols, and roles. The belief systems of disciplines will be articulated and complemented by colleagues across the clinical teams.

Questions for Discussion

1. Cultural leadership requires communication from all levels of an organization. What might be some "normal" obstacles to this requirement in traditional bureaucratic health care systems?
2. Culture is carried by the individual. Culture is based on beliefs and values. What impact does cultural leadership have on the interviewing, hiring, and orientation procedures of a nursing department or unit?
3. Language reflects and influences collective understandings among members of an organization. How would a prospective candidate for a staff nurse position assess the culture of a nursing care unit?
4. Cognitive transformation is a key skill of cultural leadership. Discuss practical application in the six areas discussed in this chapter that are of primary concern for the cultural leader.
5. Sense making helps the membership of an organization or unit to

maintain equilibrium. What function does cultural leadership play in assuring adequate sense making?

References

Bennis, W. and Nanus, B. (1985). *Leaders: the strategies for taking charge*. New York: Harper & Row.

Burns, J.M. (1979). *Leadership*. New York: Harper & Row.

Calhoun, G. (1989). A view from the top: an organizational perspective. *Nurse Managers' Bookshelf, 1* (1), 105-114.

Cameron, K.S. and Whetton, D.A. (1983). Models of the organizational life cycle: applications to higher education. *The Review of Higher Education, 6* (4), 269-299.

Clemens, J.K. and Mayer, D.F. (1987). *The classic touch: lessons in leadership from Homer to Hemingway*. Homewood, Ill.: Dow Jones-Irwin.

Curtin, Leah (1989). Hospitals 1990: back to the future . . . or else! *Nursing Management, 20* (12), 7-8.

Deal, T.E. and Kennedy, A.A. (1982). *Corporate cultures: the rites and rituals of corporate life*. Reading, Mass.: Addison-Wesley Publishing Company, Inc., Mass.

Denison, D.R. and Mishra, A.K. (1989). Organizational culture and organizational effectiveness: a theory and some preliminary empirical evidence. *Best Papers Proceedings Academy of Management*. Forty-Ninth Annual Meeting. Washington, D.C.

Harris, S. (1989). A scheme-based perspective on organizational culture. *Best Papers Proceedings Academy of Management*. Forty-Ninth Annual Meeting. Washington, D.C.

Kaluzney, A.D. (1989). Revitalizing decision making at the middle management level. *Hospital & Health Services Administration, 34* (1), 39-51.

Kilmann, R.H. (1989). *Managing beyond the quick fix*. San Francisco: Jossey-Bass Publishers.

Kilmann, R.H. and Saxton, M.J. (1983). *Kilmann-Saxton culture-gap survey*. Pittsburgh: Organizational Design Consultants, Incorporated.

Louis, M.R. (1980). Surprise and sense making: what newcomers experience in entering unfamiliar organizational settings. *Administrative Science Quarterly, 25*, 226-251.

Maanen, J.V. and Barley, S.R. (1985). Cultural organization: fragments of a theory, ed. Frost, P.J. et al, *Organizational Culture*. Beverly Hills: Sage Publications, 31-53.

Meyer, B.T. and Merrell, D.W. (1984). The life cycle of the organization-part 1. *The Journal of Commercial Bank Lending, 9*, 37.

Nanus, B. (1989). *The leader's edge: the seven keys to leadership in a turbulent world*. Chicago: Contemporary Books.

Peters, T.J. and Waterman, R.H. (1982). *In search of excellence: lessons from America's best-run companies.* New York: Warner Books.

Pettigrew, A.M. (1979). On studying organizational cultures. *Administrative Science Quarterly, 24,* 570-581.

Schein, E.H. (1985). *Organizational culture and leadership.* San Francisco: Jossey-Bass Publishers.

Smircich, L. (1983). Concepts of culture and organizational analysis. *Administrative Science Quarterly, 28,* 339-358.

Wilkins, A.L. (1983). The culture audit: a tool for understanding organizations. *Organizational Dynamics,* Autumn, 1983, 24-38.

Zaleznik, A. (1989). *The managerial mystique: restoring leadership in business.* New York: Harper & Row.

IV

Deployment of Self

6

MARY JO BOEGLIN

Shared Governance

CHAPTER OBJECTIVES

☐ State the environmental factors favoring the development of a shared governance model.

☐ State the major goals of shared governance.

☐ Identify the key characteristics for a model of shared governance.

☐ Differentiate between the concepts of shared governance and participatory management.

☐ Differentiate between decentralization within a bureaucratic structure and shared governance.

During the past decade, shared governance has been introduced as an alternative to the traditional power structures found within most institutional settings. Although many different models of shared governance have evolved, they all have one theme in common: the empowerment of staff nurses (Trofino, 1989). Shared governance allows each staff nurse an equal vote in major nursing practice decisions (Sullivan and Decker, 1988) and is seen as a means for changing the practice of nursing from subservient to autonomous (Ludemann and Brown, 1989). Staff empowerment is the premise upon which transformational leadership is based (Bennis and Nanus, 1985).

The decade of the 1980s began and ended with a nursing shortage. Around the mid-1980s the shortage appeared to be abating, but the reality of a significant shortage of registered nurses later resurfaced, becoming a major force exerting pressure on the health care system (Fine, 1989).

In 1989 the number of nursing graduates was at its lowest level since 1973 (Department of Health and Human Services, 1988). Nursing once was one of a very limited number of occupations from which a woman could choose. This is no longer the case. Nursing now has to compete with an almost unlimited number of occupations for women, and it has not been very successful in attracting men into its numbers. There is also a decreasing number of high school graduates — the traditional source of potential students — who are interested in the profession. Nursing must improve its professional image to attract new candidates (Porter, Porter, and Lower, 1989).

The nursing shortage has increased the need to examine organizational structures to improve the recruitment and retention of registered nurses (Fine, 1989). There are currently more registered nurses actively employed in nursing than at any previous time, but there also are more nurse vacancies (DHHS, 1988). Replacing a nurse with another nurse is no longer a simple matter. Nurse retention and the impact of structures, management, and leadership on the nursing staff are important issues that must be faced if the nursing shortage is to be combated effectively (Marriner, 1982, p. 97).

More than two-thirds of the active registered nurses in the United States are employed by hospitals (DHHS, 1988). Shidler, Pencak, and McFolling (1989) are supported by Aydelotte (1983) in stating that the unattractiveness of the hospital as a work setting has contributed to the shortage of nurses. Nurses have expressed strong dissatisfaction with the lack of autonomy found in the hospital setting (American Hospital Association, 1987). Conflict exists between the ideal of autonomous professional practice and the powerlessness experienced by nurses in a hospital setting.

Autonomy is generally recognized as a key attribute of a profession, but a bureaucratic organizational structure prevents autonomous practice. In most hospitals, nurses are assigned significant responsibilities without an opportunity to have input into nursing care decisions. The nurse's self-perception of being a professional is countered by an administration that views the nurse as an employee (Aydelotte, 1983).

The dual roles of nurses as employees and professionals do not have to conflict. Although there is overlap in authority and responsibilities between an employed professional and the employer, a setting can be established to support the nurse as a professional by replacing the bureaucratic model with a shared power model (Curtain, 1987).

The increased autonomy inherent in a shared governance structure leads to increased accountability, which can be overwhelming to the nursing staff. Additionally, the role of the manager in a shared governance structure must be learned (McDonagh, Rhodes, Sharkey and Goodroe, 1989). The traditional management functions of directing and controlling are not the same in a shared governance system as in a bureaucratic system. A supportive leadership and management style is necessary to coach the staff to accept accountability for nursing practice and facilitate the development of future nurse leaders. Nurse managers must be secure in the leadership role and should not view the empowerment of staff nurses as an erosion of their own responsibilities or power base. In fact, Bass's (1990) description of transformational leadership describes a supportive leader who acts as a coach or mentor to his or her followers.

There is a parallel between the governance at many universities and the organizational structure being sought in hospital settings. In the academic setting, faculty have primary responsibility for the areas of curriculum, instruction, faculty status, and the academic aspects of student life but do recognize the legal authority of the board and president. The autonomous focus of professional authority and the reluctance of professionals to accept adminis-trative authority require that higher education take a different approach to the problems of management and governance (Birnbaum, 1989, p. 14).

A shared governance model, however, does not alter the legal responsibility of either the nurse or the employer. A legal sharing of responsibility already exists for nurses and their employers. In an employed situation, the *respondeat superior* doctrine can subject the nurse's employer to liability for the nurse's act of negligence. When an employer can be held liable, the employer has a legal right to exercise direction and control over the employee's actions. However, the *respondeat superior* doctrine does not relieve the nurse of liability. As a professional, a nurse can still be held legally responsible. That responsibility goes beyond the nurse's direct action to include negligence as well as failure to report other team members' incompetence, negligence, or dangerous acts (Bernzweig, 1990).

Shared Governance

Nurses are increasingly demanding autonomy, accountability, and authority in their practice (New and New, 1989). To achieve full professional status, a group must exercise autonomy within its defined area of practice. Governance refers to the establishment and maintenance of social, political, and economic arrangements by which practitioners maintain control over their practice, self-discipline, working conditions, and professional affairs (Aydelotte, 1983). Power and authority are reflections of autonomy, so there can be no autonomy without governance.

Shared governance offers nurses power, control, and autonomy over their professional practice within an institutional setting. Authority, accountability, and the capacity for decision making are central features of shared governance. There is no single model of shared governance nor uniformity in its terminology (Wilson, 1989). Some of the structures referred to as shared governance models are missing one or more of the central features of shared governance. There are also alternate terms such as "shared power models" (Aydelotte, 1983; Shidler et al., 1989) and "professional practice models" (Lassiter, 1989; Wilcoxon, 1989) that provide autonomous nursing practice. A careful review of various models is necessary to identify a true model of shared governance.

In shared governance, staff nurses participate in the decisions regarding nursing practice and the practice setting. The nursing staff specifies the clinical skills required of staff nurses and uses peer review to monitor nurse practice. Through shared governance, staff nurses assume decision-making authority and accountability for nursing practice (Porter-O'Grady, 1989).

In the traditional bureaucratic organization, a committee structure acts in an advisory capacity to management. Management retains the power for decision making. In a shared governance model, a group structure is developed to assume the power and accountability for decision making (Porter-O'Grady and Finnigan, 1984, pp. 84-85). According to Porter-O'Grady and Finnigan (1984), autonomy and accountability for establishing policy and participating in planning are fundamental to the professional's role (p. 53), and a democratic framework helps to reduce hindrances to professional nursing practice (p. 55). A decentralized structure and a participative style of leadership are necessary to create an environment for shared governance.

A participative environment lays a foundation for shared governance but does not ensure a shared governance structure. Participation can be interpreted to imply that the staff nurses make suggestions, offer ideas, and have input while management has the ultimate power of decision. In shared governance, staff nurses actually have the power to vote in decision making. The empowerment of staff nurses is believed to be a critical factor in shared governance models (Ludemann and Brown, 1989).

Empowerment, accountability, and responsibility are basic concepts in transformational leadership (Cottingham, 1988). In transformational leadership, the leader is responsible for creating a work environment that promotes staff development. According to Bass (1990), superior performance occurs when the transformational leader can stimulate and inspire individuals to move beyond individual interests to accept the interests of the group.

Shared Governance Models

The changes involved in moving toward a shared governance structure are incremental. For a structure that previously has not vested power to front line managers, changing that policy is a first step toward participative management. Townsend's (1990) report on Kaiser Permanente Medical Center in Anaheim, California, illustrates the point. After a staff survey on job satisfaction indicated structural weaknesses within the division of nursing, a participative process was used to plan and implement a structural reorganization. Initially, all top level nurse managers met to build consensus regarding the divisional needs. Budgetary constraints, coupled with the nursing philosophy, led to a major redesign of the organizational structure. To ensure acceptance of the new structure, the entire management team was included in defining the new roles in operational terms. Although the new structure required a change of position for 70% of the nurse managers, they were all retained. The successful implementation of the new nursing structure was attributed to the participative approach.

A more developed model exists at the John Hopkins Hospital (Wilcoxon, 1989). The unit-based shared governance model gives the nursing staff control and accountability for nursing practice. Scheduling, staffing standards, quality assurance, and role definitions are all generated by the staff at the unit level.

A highly centralized structure is not conducive to autonomy. A decentralized structure is necessary for staff nurses to control nursing practice at the unit level (Fennell, 1989). Decentralization is necessary for, but not a guarantee of, a model of shared governance.

At Duke University Medical Center, the nursing turnover rate in an intensive care unit was reduced from 50% to 24% over a 5-year period by decentralizing staffing. Self-staffing was instituted to place all staffing decisions at the unit level. The unit manager, rather than the covering house supervisor, assumed responsibility for the unit's staffing. Committees were formed for staff input, but nursing management maintained the power and control of decision making. A survey of the staff indicated 100% of the staff believed that self-staffing enhanced patient care, 99% thought that it enhanced unit morale, and 94% noted improved job satisfaction (Martin et al., 1989).

No single nursing care delivery model is considered essential to shared governance. The central theme in a shared governance model is the accountability of the nursing staff. A primary nursing model is favored by many institutions, whereas an integrated approach is favored by others.

Three patient-care delivery models received attention at Tucson Medical Center: Managed Care/Case Management, Differentiated Practice, and Primary Nursing. Components from each of the three were integrated and then incorporated with the concept of staff empowerment. A nurse case manager is assigned to each patient and is accountable for the patient care outcomes for the entire illness episode (Del Togno-Armanasco et al., 1989).

There are numerous examples of shared governance in the literature. Some are in early stages of development, while others are well developed. Several of those in the early stages have been described previously. Four examples of developed models follow.

The Rush-Presbyterian-St. Luke's Medical Center governance structure was designed to bring nursing into parity with hospital administration and medicine. Primary nursing, a clinical ladder, and decentralized decision making formed a foundation that enabled nursing to move toward its goal of self-governance. The planning that led the nursing staff to develop a self-governance structure was initiated in the late 1970s. Responsibility and accountability for patient care is placed directly on the practicing nurses. The existing management system supported the philosophy that nurses' responsibility and accountability for patient care paralleled that of the medical staff. The professional nursing staff was involved from the inception of the idea to its implementation in 1984. The Professional Nursing Staff (PNS) is made up of all of the professional nurses—caregivers and managers alike—who are employed in the six clinical departments comprising the division of nursing. The PNS is founded on the premise that all of the nurses throughout the institution are recognized as professionals and are accountable for the quality of care within the institution. Advisory committees provide a forum in which staff nurses contribute to the decision-making process, but the nurse manager is ultimately responsible and maintains final decision-making authority. A department advisory committee (DAC) participates in policy decisions and advises the department chair. The unit advisory committee (UAC) is the key to autonomy. Through the UAC, staff nurses can directly influence and shape nursing practice on their units (Shidler et al., 1989).

St. Joseph's Hospital of Atlanta was in its eighth year of shared governance when McDonagh, Rhodes, Sharkey, and Goodroe (1989) wrote their article about it. Adhering to the emphasis on individual professional accountability, the hospital requires that all members of the professional nursing staff are registered nurses. The staff nurse, or clinical practitioner, is the focus of the shared governance structure. Support positions exist and operate to support the professional staff nurse. The professional practice model philosophy of shared governance contrasts with the hospital's bureaucratic structure, but it is supported in the corporate organization by nursing and hospital administration. Professional collaboration, rather than a chain of command, is emphasized. The standards of practice developed by the professional nursing organization offer guidance for professional judgment. There are five major nursing councils: nursing management, nursing education, nursing quality assurance, nursing practice, and nursing executive; the councils collaborate to facilitate decision making. Bylaws offer legitimacy for the shared governance structure within the hospital corporation. Decisions of the shared governance structure focus on practice issues, whereas nursing administrative decisions focus on broad, hospital-based business issues. Because many decisions fall within both the administrative and professional domains, ambiguity sometimes arises regarding responsibility for certain decisions.

St. Michael's Hospital in Milwaukee has had a shared governance system evolving since 1982 (Pinkerton et al., 1989). Every member of the nursing staff belongs to a conference group. There are separate conference groups for nurse managers, clinical educators, assistant nurse managers and clinical nurse specialists, directors and assistant vice-presidents, and staff. Because of the large number of support staff, the staff conference group is represented by one member from each nursing unit. Each of the conference groups except for the staff group has one member who attends a monthly meeting of the nursing practice council (NPC); the staff conference group has five members on the NPC. The NPC makes decisions. There are also four working committees that report to the NPC. All committee recommendations are voted on by the NPC. Issues with management implications are referred to the nursing administration staff. A unit practice council (UPC) addresses unit practice issues, and its membership varies according to unit size. A staff nurse serves as chair of the UPC. The nurse manager is involved with the UPC, but participation is dependent upon the UPC structure. The UPC has the responsibility and accountability for all practice decisions on their units. Bylaws define the structure of the NPC and its membership, philosophy, purpose, and communication channels.

The University of Rochester's Strong Memorial Hospital has a Professional Nursing Organization (PNO) that places its base of power in its staff of practicing nurses. The executive committee is composed of 43 elected members, including 22 staff nurses. The staff nurse distribution is based on full-time equivalents to spread representation equally among the nursing practice groups. All members of the PNO are eligible to vote in elections. The terms for the executive committee are for 2 years, with half of the committee elected each year. The chair, vice-chair, and secretary are elected by the executive committee from within its membership. The chair assumes a voting position on the hospital's executive committee to represent nursing in executive decision making. The executive committee meets monthly and serves to keep the nursing staff in a central role regarding issues related to nursing practice. Bylaws exist, and a recent amendment was made to enhance continuity by changing the vice-chair position to chair-elect (Jones and Ortiz, 1989).

Conclusion

Staff nurses' responses to models of shared governance have been positive. Forty-one hospitals were selected for inclusion in a study authorized by the American Academy of Nursing (1983). The hospitals were selected because of their success in nurse recruitment and retention. The purpose of the study was to identify the factors associated with that success. A variety of models for nursing care delivery was found among the hospitals, but shared variables were also found. Of significant importance were environment, the model of practice, and autonomy. The nurses had the responsibility and authority for patient care.

Ludemann and Brown (1989) reported a study completed 2 years after a new governance structure was initiated at Rose Medical Center. Findings indicated that all staff perceptions were more positive after the introduction of shared governance (reliability coefficients ranged from 0.95 to 0.90). Overall job satisfaction was improved, with the greatest differences being seen on items that measured personal power, autonomy, and the climate for innovation. All of the findings were at statistically significant levels, but it was noted that generalizations could not be made from the study.

☐ *Implications for Nursing*

The number of health care facilities offering models of shared governance is increasing. Each setting has qualities unique to itself that alter the model of shared governance; no exact blueprint of shared governance exists.

The central points of shared governance are autonomy, authority, and accountability of the staff nurse for patient care. Nursing education should include more than a cursory introduction to these concepts if it is to adequately familiarize nurses with models of shared governance.

□ Application to Nursing: Case Study

Gildes Hospital, a 500-bed general hospital serving a 75-mile radius as a regional medical center, faced serious staffing problems with its professional nursing staff in 1984. A new open heart surgery program was growing rapidly, and Gildes had also been designated as the regional cancer treatment center. The occupancy rate was consistently above 90%, and patient acuity measures were high. There were staff nurse vacancies on each of the 16 nursing units, and the staff nurse turnover rate averaged 27%.

The nursing department was organized in a traditional hierarchical structure. Each of the nursing units had a head nurse who was included in staffing 60% of the time and an assistant head nurse whose primary function was as charge nurse. The nursing units were grouped into divisions, with a separate nursing supervisor in charge of each division. The nursing supervisors reported to the director of nursing (DON), who reported to the vice-president of nursing.

There were also two staff positions that reported to the vice-president of nursing. One was responsible for hiring and scheduling all professional nurses, while the other was responsible for budgeting. One nurse was responsible for the entire hospital's infection control program and reported to the DON.

Serious problems with nursing's organizational structure had been emerging for at least 2 years. The centralized scheduling was viewed by the nursing staff as autocratic and unresponsive to unit and personal needs. More importantly, decisions regarding nursing care were being made without input from the nursing staff responsible for providing that care. Significant changes became inevitable when two nursing units had to be closed because of a staff nurse shortage.

Visionary nursing leaders initiated changes that eventually led to a new organizational structure at Gildes. In the beginning stages, the urgency of the situation prevented taking the preferred collaborative approach. Scheduling and hiring were delegated to the head nurses. A direction was set for decentralization of the nursing department, but a task force was formed to develop the specific steps.

By 1989, Gildes' nursing department was decentralized, and the new structure offered an emerging model of shared governance. Staffing and budgeting for each nursing unit was under the control and responsibility of the head nurse. Each unit's nursing staff had control and accountability for the nursing care on their respective units. The staff positions for scheduling and budgeting were eliminated, as was the DON position. The six previous nurse supervisors' positions were replaced by four director positions focusing on product line management.

The changes in scope of duties resulting from the reorganization progressed slowly at times. For example, the head nurses attended classes for 6 months before assuming their budget responsibilities. At the staff level, inservice education became an on-going process to ensure understanding of the implications involved with autonomy.

Additionally, the autonomy and accountability of the nursing staff are still emerging. On the unit level staff nurses have autonomy and accountability, but on the departmental level nursing's power and authority are still vested in the vice-president of nursing by the board of directors.

Questions for Discussion

1. Briefly summarize the shared governance model created at Gildes Hospital.
2. What precepts do shared governance and transformational leadership share?
3. How did the leadership style affect the organizational structure at Gildes Hospital before the reorganization?
4. How would the new organizational structure affect the leadership style?
5. How does the model of shared governance affect autonomy?
6. What are the benefits and disadvantages for a professional nurse working within the shared governance structure of Gildes Hospital?

References

American Academy of Nursing. (1983). *Magnet hospitals: attraction and retention of professional nurses.* American Nurses Association.

American Hospital Association. (1987). *The nursing shortage: facts, figures, and feelings* (AHA No. 154100). Chicago, Ill: The Association.

Aydelotte, M. K. (1983). Professional nursing: The drive for governance. In N. L. Chaska, editor: *The nursing profession: a time to speak* (pp. 830-843). New York: McGraw-Hill.

Bass, B. M. (Winter, 1990). From transactional to transformational leadership: Learnin to share the vision. *Organizational Dynamics* 18(3), 19-31.

Bennis, W. & Nanus, B. (1985). *Leaders: The strategies for taking charge.* New York: Harper & Row.

Bernzweig, E. P. (1990). *The nurse's liability for malpractice* (ed. 5). St. Louis: Mosby-Year Book.

Birnbaum, R. (1989). *How colleges work: The cybernetics of academic organization and leadership.* San Francisco: Jossey-Bass.

Cottingham, C. (June, 1988). Transformational leadership: A strategy for nursing. *Today's O. R. Nurse, 10*(6), 24-27

Curtain, L. (1987). The employment of autonomy. *Nursing Management, 18*(3), 9-12.

Del Togno-Armanasco, V., Olivas, G. S., and Harter, S. (1989). Developing an integrated nursing case management model. *Nursing Management, 20*(10), 26-29.

Department of Health and Human Services. (1988). *1988 Sample survey of registered nurses.* Washington, DC: Division of Nursing, BHPr, HRSA, Department of Health and Human Services.

Fennell, S. E. (1989). Role of the staff nurse in developing clinical policy. *Nursing Management, 20*(1), 80I-80P.

Fine, R. B. (1989). From the transition stage to the transformed organization. In B. Henry, C. Arndt, M. DiVincenti, and A. Marriner-Tomey, editors: *Dimensions of nursing administration: Theory, research, education, practice.* Boston: Blackwell Scientific Publications.

Jones, L. S. and Ortiz, M. E. (1989). Increasing nursing autonomy and recognition through shared governance. *Nursing Administration Quarterly, 13*(4), 11-16.

Lassiter, S. S. (1989). Staff nurse retention: Strategies for success. *Journal of Neuroscience Nursing, 21*(2), 104-107.

Ludemann, R. S. and Brown, C. (1989). Staff perceptions of shared governance. *Journal of Nurse Administration, 13*(4), 19.

Marriner, A., editor: (1982). *Contemporary nursing management issues and practice.* St. Louis: Mosby-Year Book.

Martin, E. G., et al. (1989). Retention strategies that work. *Nursing Management, 20*(6), 72I, 72L-M, 72P.

McDonagh, K. J., Rhodes, B., Sharkey, K., and Goodroe, J. H. (1989). Shared governance at St. Joseph's Hospital of Atlanta: a mature professional practice model. *Nursing Administration Quarterly, 13*(4), 17-28.

New, Y. A. and New, J. R. (1989). Quality assurance that works. *Nursing Management, 20*(6), 21-24.

Pinkerton, S., et al. (1989). St. Michael Hospital: a shared governance model. *Nursing Administration Quarterly, 13*(4), 35-47.

Porter, R. T., Porter, M. J., and Lower, M. S. (1989). Enhancing the image of nursing. *Journal of Nursing Administration, 19*(2), 36-40.

Porter-O'Grady, T. (1989). Shared governance: reality or sham. *American Journal of Nursing, 89*(3), 350-351.

Porter-O'Grady, T. and Finnigan, S. (1984). *Shared governance for nursing: a creative approach to professional accountability.* Rockville, MD: Aspen Publication.

Shidler, H., et al. (1989). Professional nursing staff: a model of self-governance for nursing. *Nursing Administration Quarterly, 13*(4), 1-9.

Sullivan, E. J. and Decker, P. J. (1988). *Effective management in nursing* (ed. 2). Menlo Park, Calif.: Addison-Wesley Publishing.

Townsend, M. B. (1990). A participative approach to administrative reorganization. *Journal of Nursing Administration, 20*(2), 11-14.

Trofino, J. (1989). Empowering nurses. *Journal of Nurse Administration, 19*(4), 13.

Wilcoxon, C. E. (1989). A return to the original Nightingale concept: taking the hint. *Journal of Nurse Administration, 19*(3), 19.

Wilson, C. K. (1989). Shared governance: the challenge of change in the early phases of implementation. *Nursing Administration Quarterly, 13*(4), 29-33.

7

FATIMAH H. AL-KANDARI

Personality Styles

CHAPTER OBJECTIVES

- ☐ Discuss the trait theories of leadership.
- ☐ Identify the characteristics common among leaders.
- ☐ List the characteristics that followers typically admire in leaders.
- ☐ Explain the Myers-Briggs Type Indicator classifications of personality styles.

In any organization the successful achievement of goals and objectives requires the availability of effective leaders who are able to motivate co-workers. Effective leadership is the cornerstone by which the organization's success can be measured. Leaders can get extraordinary things accomplished; they are the people who challenge the process and search for opportunities.

Many leadership theories have been published over the years in an attempt to unravel the mystery of why one individual becomes a leader while another person becomes a follower. The purpose of this chapter is to provide an overview of leadership trait theories and to discuss the personality styles and characteristics of leaders.

Gibson, Ivancevich, and Donnelly (1985, p. 362) defined leadership as "an attempt to use noncoercive types of influence to motivate individuals to accomplish some goals." Couture (1986, p. 36) used a similar definition, describing the leader in the sports world as "the guy who provides direction, goals, tools, and tactics. He's an organized thinker with a long-term perspective and a plan to get there. He's the unselfish person who gives his players the knowledge and the support that can make them winners."

Characteristics of Leaders

Until the mid-1940s trait theory was the dominant leadership theory. Early research indicated that individuals inherit certain traits that make them leaders. However, later work in this area suggested that traits can be acquired through learning and experience. Hence, research efforts were directed toward identifying intellectual, emotional, physical, and other personal traits of successful leaders (Gibson et al., 1985). A long list shows some of, but not all, of the identified traits (Marriner-Tomey, 1992, pp. 261-263; Gibson et al., 1985, p. 366):

Adaptability	Emotional stability	Knowledge
Affection	Energy	Loyalty
Aggressiveness	Enthusiasm	Popularity
Alertness	Fairness	Prestige
Ambition	Friendliness	Self-assurance
Decisiveness	Honesty	Self-confidence

Dependability	Independence	Teaching ability
Diplomacy	Individuality	Technical mastery
Drive	Interpersonal skills	

In *The Leadership Challenge,* Kouzes and Posner (1988) have identified some specific characteristics that are common among leaders. The authors indicated that leaders typically use skills such as challenging the process, inspiring a shared vision, enabling others to act, modeling the way, and encouraging the heart.

Challenging the process involves searching for opportunities and taking risks. Kouzes and Posner defined leaders as pioneers who are willing to step into the unknown. They are not afraid of innovation or experimentation. They try different things to discover new ways of accomplishing the task at hand. The two authors called leaders "early adopters of innovation." The underlying concept of challenging the process is change. Regardless of the organization or the task at hand, leaders are not afraid to make changes. They usually challenge the status quo and question the routine. Without change and without people willing to take risks, crises would never be resolved and there probably never would have been any revolutionary movements or social transformations. Leaders search for opportunities and take risks themselves, and they also encourage their followers to innovate and become risk-takers. Leaders encourage their followers not to be afraid of failure. The fear of failure acts as a self-imposed constraint that often blocks people from innovating and changing.

The second characteristic of leaders is the ability to inspire a shared vision. Leaders look to the future, and the inspired vision usually evokes pictures and images of the future. Therefore an inspired vision "is an ideal and unique image of the future" (Kouzes and Posner, 1988, p. 84). Nevertheless, leaders are aware that a vision must be shared because they cannot accomplish all the work by themselves. Attracting others and developing a shared vision is a key characteristic. Many years ago, Napoleon Bonaparte realized the importance of shared vision and said, "The only way to lead people is to show them a future: a leader is a dealer in hope" (Lippitt, 1987, p. 265). Roberts agreed with Kouzes and Posner's description and indicated that "visionary goal-setting is what leadership is all about" (1989, p. 30). He also wrote that true leaders are those who can convince others to buy their visions and dreams. Leaders communicate frequently with their followers to discover common purpose and to bring common purpose and vision to life. Leaders very often succeed in enlisting others by appealing to the followers' values, interests, hopes, and dreams.

Enabling others to act is another leadership characteristic discussed by Kouzes and Posner (1988). Leaders actively involve others in planning, implementing, and decision-making. Leaders, in their attempt to enable others to act, strengthen their colleagues' abilities and foster collaboration among them.

Leaders develop collaborative goals and emphasize cooperation rather than competition among co-workers. Leaders also enlarge their followers' sphere of influence and give them visibility and recognition, helping them to feel autonomous, important, and trustworthy.

The fourth characteristic is modeling the way. Leaders set the example for others by behaving in ways that are consistent with their values (Kouzes and Posner, 1988). Values are fundamentally important to human beings. "They are the deep-seated, persuasive standards that influence almost every aspect of our lives, our moral judgements, our response to others, our commitments to personal and organizational goals" (Kouzes and Posner, 1988, p. 190). Followers observe the leader's actions in critical situations and during periods of evaluation and reward. From observing their leader's behavior, followers determine whether to trust their leader and whether the leader's overall message conflicts with or agrees with the leader's verbalized message. Leaders also model the way by building a commitment to action. This commitment can be achieved by providing people with opportunities to make meaningful, permanent choices and by giving public recognition to followers' accomplishments. In brief, leaders become the role models by which followers pattern their behaviors and actions.

The last characteristic is encouraging the heart. Getting extraordinary tasks accomplished is not a simple matter. Followers need motivation to enhance their progress and push them forward toward reaching their goals. Leaders are aware of this fact, and they tend to recognize individuals' contributions and celebrate accomplishments so that followers become and remain motivated. Rewarding behavior and celebrating accomplishments are important; followers learn which actions are rewarded and which are not, so they direct their efforts toward the rewarded behaviors. Tyagi (1985) conducted a research study on the relative importance of key job dimensions and leadership behaviors in motivating the work performance of salespeople. Tyagi found that leadership behavior was influential in affecting workers' extrinsic motivation, while key job dimensions (such as love of the work) were more influential in affecting the workers' intrinsic motivation.

Flexibility and clear thinking during crises are two additional critical characteristics for today's leaders, according to Barr and Barr (1989). They described the leader as a person who "is more fearless, more clear, more unlimited, more wise, and more courageous than anyone else around" (Barr and Barr, 1989, p. 6). Bennis (1988) reported ten behavioral traits possessed by distinguished leaders: self-knowledge, openness to feedback, eagerness to learn and improve, curiosity and risk-taking, concentration on work, ability to learn from adversity, balance of tradition and change, open style of work, ability to work well with systems, and ability to serve as models and mentors.

The frequently observed characteristics and behavioral traits of leaders agree to some extent with characteristics that followers admire and expect in their leaders. Followers usually admire leaders who are honest, competent, forward-looking, and inspirational; all of these traits put together make the leader credible (Kouzes and Posner, 1988).

Myers-Briggs Type Indicator

Catherine C. Briggs and her daughter, Isabel Briggs Myers, were researchers who were very interested in human behavior. Their interest resulted in developing the Myers-Briggs Type Indicator, based on Jung's theory of personality. It identifies human behavior and personality styles in four dimensions, each of which has two categories (Table 7-1). The instrument is a helpful tool for on-going self-examination and has been used by many researchers interested in studying leaders' and followers' personality styles.

Barr and Barr (1989), who have administered the Myers-Briggs Type Indicator to thousands of managers and executives, indicated that leaders must develop excellence in all eight areas to sustain consistent leadership. Each type has its strengths and weaknesses; understanding this point can lead to fulfillment and effective leadership.

Life attitude is the first dimension, and its two categories are extroversion and introversion. This dimension refers to the communication style by which people interact and transmit information. The two categories follow Carl Jung's definitions. Extroversion describes a process that focuses primarily on the external world of people and activities, whereas introversion is more inwardly focused on concepts and ideas (Barr and Barr, 1989).

In terms of the work environment, extroverts tend to move around the organization more, and they like more casual conversation. They are energized by stimuli from the external environment. Talkative, outgoing, and sociable, they prefer interaction. Extroverts react to stress primarily by increasing activity. They make decisions quickly, are able to switch gears easily, and do not mind interruptions.

Introverts, on the other hand, tend to concentrate more on the work in their office. They probe deeply into issues, interact selectively, and are reflective, calm, and quiet. They discriminate clearly between acquaintances and friends, and they are territorial. Introverts react to stress primarily by decreasing activity. They gather information thoroughly, develop ideas well, and make well-formulated decisions. They persuade others by using sound logic (Barr and Barr, 1989).

In this dimension, differences between people in organizations, especially between followers and their leader(s), can result in conflicts. For this reason leaders who have a preference for one category usually develop the ability to function in the other category as well.

The two dimensions of perception and judgement, with their respective categories of sensing or intuiting and thinking or feeling, are considered communication channels for shaping messages. *Sensing* and *intuiting* are the

Table 7-1 **Personality Styles**

Dimensions		Categories
Life attitude	=	Extroversion or introversion
Perception	=	Sensing or intuiting
Judgement	=	Thinking or feeling
Outer world orientation	=	Judging or perceiving

ways of perceiving messages, and *thinking* and *feeling* are the ways of judging what is perceived.

An individual's preference for sensory or intuitive information affects how that person sees the world. Usually people with a strong preference for the sensory category "prefer real world information that can be verified by their five senses" (Barr and Barr, 1989, p. 3). They are also good at recognizing and fixing what is not working well. They prefer specific tasks with specific payoffs, and they develop systematic procedures for accomplishing the work. Practical, realistic, and result-oriented, they dislike change, ambiguity, and long-range planning. Some characteristic strengths of sensors include the following: wanting observable facts, and step-by-step explanations; preferring the tried and the tested; demanding proof; liking to get things done; and thriving on competition. The sensors' weaknesses are several: they may overlook implications and meanings; they may not see the guiding principle behind the information; they may reject new, innovative ideas, preferring obsolete methods or techniques; they might miss opportunities while waiting for proof; and they may push too hard, doing things too quickly out of a fondness for competition and even competing over unimportant issues.

Intuitors, on the contrary, prefer to interpret information according to its "meaning, possibility, and implication" (Barr and Barr, 1989, p. 3). They are more future-oriented with little focus on today. They also focus on what someone means, whereas sensors focus on what someone says. In addition, intuitors can recognize things that could lead to future problems. They are idealistic and abstract, and they consider various possibilities. Liking variety and challenge, they are imaginative and dislike a great deal of structure. Intuitors' strengths include the following: thinking quickly; using "big picture" thinking while synthesizing random data; seeing possibilities and recognizing patterns; being visionary and individualistic; working productively on bursts of energy; developing systems for doing work; and having the ability to read between the lines. Intuitors are weak in these respects: they may skim information and miss essential data; they may leave things dangling and become unfocused; they can be impractical and egocentric; they may become bored easily; and they can be unrealistic about the time required to accomplish tasks.

Thinking and feeling are the categories by which people judge what they see. According to Barr and Barr (1989), people perceive through sensing-intuiting channels and then make decisions about perceptions through thinking-feeling channels. Thinkers usually make judgements about the information based on rationality; they value logical organization, preferring an objective approach to performing a job; they appear to be head-dominated; and they explain things thoroughly, preferring to make remarks that are objective and impersonal. Some of the thinkers' strengths are seen in favoring analytical and logical expression; valuing logic; handling emergencies logically; and preferring a formal approach. Among their weaknesses, on the other hand, they may undervalue feelings in motivating people; they may appear cold and insensitive; they may over-explain and ask too many questions; and they can be overly formal.

Feelers usually make judgements with the personal side of the information in mind; they appear to be heart-dominated and supportive of others; they exhibit emotional sensitivity and like to communicate. The dominant feelers' strengths include supporting and giving to others; sharing emotional sensitivity with others; seeing the personal perspective and interpreting events as they affect humans; desiring to communicate; and, identifying with people's feelings, freely overextending themselves to help others.

The feelers' weaknesses consist of these things: they may give and support indiscriminately; they can become overloaded with feelings that distort perception; they may give away too much information, overreact, and hold grudges. Just as it is necessary to balance between extroversion and introversion and between sensing and intuiting, leaders must also balance between thinking and feeling.

The last dimension, outer world orientation, consists of the two categories of judging and perceiving. These two categories affect the way people control aspects of their lives. Individuals characterized as judging have a desire to evaluate, plan, organize and maximize their use of time; have strong ideas about how things should be performed; want to get things done promptly and move on to new tasks; prefer to work in a steady, planned way; like a sense of closure; want to control time, prefer advance notice and strict schedules; are decisive and goal-oriented; and prefer to use the judgement channels of thinking as the dominant channel of communication for shaping messages.

Perceiving individuals typically desire to "hang loose"; control their own participation; enjoy spontaneous challenges; work in a flexible, informal way; discover tasks and manage them as they occur rather than planning for them; obtain ample information to explore more options; understand and use processes; and use the communicating channels of sensing or intuiting as the dominant channels for shaping messages.

From the four dimensions and eight categories, 16 possible personality styles exist. The Myers-Briggs Type Indicator classifies people according to these combinations. For example, if a person's personality style is classified "ESTJ," it means that his or her dominant preferences are extroversion, sensing, thinking, and judging. To become a successful leader, this individual should develop the flexibility to function as well in his or her less-preferred categories: introversion, intuition, feeling, and perception (Barr and Barr, 1989; Myers and Myers, 1980).

In business firms, leadership ability has received considerable attention. Transformational and entrepreneurial leaders are those who are capable of energizing themselves and others toward reaching goals and going beyond the expected (Lippitt, 1987). According to Williams (1980), at least six behavioral characteristics of the transformational or entrepreneurial leader seem relevant to small business firms. These behavioral characteristics are risk-taking, divergent thinking, sharp focus on clearly defined objectives, personal responsibility (internal locus of control), economic orientation, and the ability to learn from experience.

Research on entrepreneurship provides behavioral characteristics of the entrepreneurial leader in addition to those mentioned by Williams (1980). Lippitt (1987) summarized research findings on this topic and listed characteristics such as "high drive and energy level; self-confidence; long-term involvement in work goals (5 to 7 years); using money as a measure (not an end); persistent at solving problems; setting challenging and realistic goals; taking moderate risks; learning from but not being discouraged by failure; responding constructively to criticism; and taking initiative and seeking personal responsibility" (p. 268).

Fernald (1988) provided examples of leadership behaviors and characteristics that were identified by Williams and Lippitt. One example shows the case of Steve Woziak. Woziak had had no intention of starting a company before he and Steve Jobs started designing and building Apple computer in the mid-1970s. It all started with an idea, a vision that was cherished and that received undevoted attention. Characteristics such as determination, risk, vision, and perseverance played a major role in their success and in nurturing their idea. Woziak and Jobs built their first computer in Jobs' garage. Woziak sold two of his Hewlett-Packard calculators and Jobs sold his Volkswagen bus in order to be able to finance their business. Woziak resigned from his job so that he could work on the computer. He took a risk by not having a steady income, and there was a possibility of failure. Nevertheless, the risks did not stop him or his partner from being forward-looking and persistent. Their cherished vision and inspiration for designing a computer made them successful in the business market. In the mid-1970s the design was finished and by 1980 their sales topped $100 million (Fernald, 1988).

The case of Helen Smith is another example of demonstrated leadership behavior and risk-taking. Sales of her famous pies reached $137,000 by the end of the first year of business. Helen Smith had worked as a secretary for 27 years until a fire destroyed her employer's business and she was without a job. She lived on food stamps and welfare for about 3 years to support herself and her three children. Helen had confidence in her baking abilities, so she went to five local restaurants, asking them if they would market her homemade pies until she could find a steady job. The restaurants agreed, and the pies sold well. She found a job as a secretary for a Houston oil company, but her former customers continued asking for pies and encouraged her to open a pie shop. After 3 years of working with the oil company she quit her job and took the risk of supporting her family without a regular paycheck. She enrolled in a Small Business Administration seminar and applied for a loan to establish a pie selling business. Helen's 5-year goals included projected sales of $100,000 by the end of the fifth year. Astonishingly, she sold approximately $137,000 worth of pies by the end of the first year. Helen said her secret for success was hard work, determination, and belief in herself and in her ability (Fernald, 1988).

American presidents comprise a group of leaders whose personality styles receive more attention than any other category of leaders (Simonton, 1988). Although it is not easy to identify the individual traits that contribute to presidential success, presidents' personality styles were analyzed in terms of five categories: the interpersonal, charismatic, deliberative, creative, and neurotic styles.

Interpersonal presidents have been seen to remain flexible; contact cabinet members frequently but allow them considerable independence; encourage independent judgement; and maintain close relationships with co-workers.

The charismatic president was found to be a skilled and self-confident negotiator; one who kept in contact with the public; one who was full of energy and determination; one who was rarely shy; and one who continually was refining his public image.

The deliberative president exhibited characteristics such as understanding the implications of his decisions; showing depth of comprehension; being able to visualize alternatives and weigh long-term consequences; and displaying caution and conservativeness in action.

Creative presidents initiated a lot of new legislation and programs and demonstrated innovation in the role of executive. The neurotic president placed political success over effective policy and suffered health problems correlated to difficult and critical periods in office. He almost never used a direct, uncomplicated approach.

Simonton's (1988) research findings revealed that although a president might be characterized by a single style, many presidents display more than one dimension or style. To summarize the characteristics of each style, the interpersonal presidents were found to be good-natured, pleasant, easy going, and trusting; the charismatic presidents were outgoing, natural, and witty; the deliberative presidents were organized, insightful, polished, methodical, intelligent, and sophisticated; the creative presidents were inventive and artistic; and the neurotic presidents were found to be evasive (Simonton, 1988). Furthermore, the analysis revealed that John Kennedy scored high on charisma and deliberative and creative styles. Lyndon Johnson scored positively on charisma, although he scored the highest on neuroticism of all twentieth century presidents. Franklin Roosevelt and Andrew Jackson scored at the top of the list for charismatic and deliberative styles. Ronald Reagan scored somewhat higher on creativity than on interpersonal or deliberative styles. Thomas Jefferson scored high on creativity but low on charisma; whereas the reverse was seen in Theodore Roosevelt. Simonton (1988) concluded his study by indicating that a president who scores high in interpersonal style or charisma seems to be person-oriented, whereas the deliberative and creative presidents appear to be more task-oriented.

☐ Implications for Nursing

A transformational nursing leader is one who challenges the process, searches for opportunities, inspires a shared vision, enables others to act, models the way, and encourages the heart. Nursing leaders should know their dominant traits, develop the weaker ones, and maintain a balance within the categories of extroversion and introversion, sensing and intuiting, thinking and feeling, and judging and perceiving. It is also useful for the nursing leader to know the followers' dominant styles, to develop teams with a variety of strengths and weaknesses, and to use those strengths to maximize excellence.

☐ Application to Nursing: Case Study

Nancy is a clinical nurse who works in an acute care setting. She is a very sociable and talkative person, expressive of her thoughts, feelings, and ideas. Nancy dislikes structure, stimulates communication among peers, and clinically is very skillful. Sometimes she becomes egocentric, does not like to assist others when they need help, over-reacts to situations, and holds grudges against others if something goes wrong.

Her direct supervisor, Francis, is a patient care coordinator (PCC) and has a personality style different from Nancy's. Francis is more calm and quiet, less talkative, and very organized and structured; she prefers to evaluate, plan, organize, and maximize her use of time. She gathers information thoroughly and, as their performance evaluator, observes the nurses' actions very carefully.

At the time of Nancy's 90-day evaluation, Francis told Nancy that she liked her nursing skills. However, she indicated the need to become more structured, less talkative, and less manipulative. She also told her that she needed to be careful about her style of sometimes imposing her ideas and thoughts on other people because that could cause problems. She explained that not many people on the unit like to receive ideas from others. Nancy was surprised about what she heard and told Francis that she would try to become less talkative and more structured. Nancy left the office upset about what she heard and decided to leave the unit as soon as her contract expired.

Questions for Discussion

1. What do you think is Nancy's personality style?
2. What do you think is Francis's personality style?
3. What does the PCC need to consider when working with Nancy?
4. Do you see any potential for personality conflict? If yes, what kind?

References

Barr, L. and Barr, N. (1989). *The leadership equation. Leadership, management, and the Myers-Briggs.* Austin, Tex.: Eakin Press.

Bennis, W. (1988). Ten traits of dynamic leaders. *Executive Excellence, 5* (2), 8-9.

Couture, G. (1986). Fast track to leadership? *Manage, 38* (3), 26-27.

Fernald, L.W. (1988). The underlying relationship between creativity, innovation, and entrepreneurship. *The Journal of Creative Behavior, 22* (3), 196-202.

Gibson, J., Ivancevich, J., and Donnelly, J. (1985). *Organizations behavior. Structure-processes.* (ed. 5). Plano, Tex.: Business Publications.

Kouzes, J.M., and Posner, B.Z. (1988). *The leadership challenge.* San Francisco: Jossey-Bass.

Lippitt, G. (1987). Entrepreneurial leadership: A performing art. *The Journal of Creative Behavior, 21* (3), 264-270.

Marriner-Tomey, A. (1988). *Guide to nursing management.* St. Louis: Mosby-Year Book.

Myers, I.B.M. and Myers, P.B. (1980). *Gifts differing.* Palo Alto, Calif.: Consulting Psychologists Press.

Roberts, R.J. (1989). Vision and leadership. *Canadian Banker, 96* (2), 30-33.

Simonton, D.K. (1988). Presidential style: Personality, biography, and performance. *Journal of Personality and Social Psychology, 55* (6), 928-936.

Tyagi, P.K. (1985). Relative importance of key job dimensions and leadership behaviors in motivating salesperson work performance. *Journal of Marketing, 49* (3), 76-86.

Williams, H.S. (1980). Entrepreneurs in the nonprofit world. *Business, 2*(4)

8

JUDITH A. HALSTEAD

Leader As Socializer

CHAPTER OBJECTIVES

- ☐ Define organizational socialization.
- ☐ Describe the role of the leader in the organizational socialization process.
- ☐ Discuss the process of vicarious learning, or role modeling, as defined within the framework of Bandura's social learning theory.
- ☐ Describe the potential effects of vicarious learning, or role modeling, on the development of organizational behavior.
- ☐ Analyze the leader's role in utilizing the modeling process to influence the development of organizational behavior.
- ☐ Apply the process of vicarious learning, or role modeling, to nursing leadership and development of organizational behavior within a nursing service setting.

S ocialization is a very important process within an organization. Through effective socialization efforts an organization is able to enhance the performance of its individuals and groups and ultimately improve the performance of the organization (Gibson, Ivancevich, and Donnelly, 1982). This chapter discusses organizational socialization and the leader's role as a model in providing effective socialization experiences for individuals employed within the organization. Social learning theory (Bandura, 1977b) provides the framework upon which this discussion is based.

Organizational Socialization

"As soon as she learns the ropes around here, she will be a valuable contributor to this organization." Many of us have heard similar statements made about individuals who are new to an organization. To function effectively in new roles, individuals need to have not only ability and motivation but also a sense of what others expect of their behaviors. What values, goals, customs, or beliefs are predominant within the organization? How are such important norms and assumptions enacted within the organization? The new employee is expected to acquire an understanding and appreciation of the organizational culture. This understanding is developed through the process of organizational socialization (Louis, 1980).

Organizational socialization has been defined as "the process by which an individual comes to appreciate the values, abilities, expected behaviors, and social knowledge essential for assuming an organizational role and for participating as an organization member" (Louis, 1980, pp. 229-230). This process is most commonly thought to occur at the time of entry into an organization. Because of their concerns about being accepted and their uncertainty about what is appropriate behavior within the organization, newcomers are especially receptive to the various types of influences that constitute the socialization process. In some organizations, however, it is possible for socialization to occur throughout one's career (Pfeffer, 1982).

Socialization is a potent form of influence. If properly accomplished, individuals undergoing socialization should internalize the values of the organization. This internalization of values affects the individual's future decision-making efforts, goals, and activities (Pfeffer, 1982). Overall organiza-

114

tional performance improves as the individual's personal goals become more closely aligned with organizational goals. The ultimate purpose of socialization is to integrate the interests of the individual with those of the organization, thus enhancing the performance of both (Gibson, Ivancevich, and Donnelly, 1982).

It is important to understand that socialization will occur within an organization whether or not it is planned (Gibson et al., 1982). The individual's daily interactions with managers and peers provide a form of social influence through which expectations and values are conveyed. To ensure that socialization is effective and appropriate, individuals should be exposed to the specific values, beliefs, customs, and behaviors considered acceptable within the organization's culture. The leaders within the organization have a vital role in this process.

Bennis and Nanus (1985) stated that serving as a model for followers may be one of the most important roles a leader can assume. Leaders are models that symbolize the identity and unity of a group (Gardner, 1986). As such, a leader's behavior can be critical in determining what values are promoted and defended within an organization. In their personal interactions with others, leaders can demonstrate their commitment to the organization's values. Effective transformational leaders consider how values can be reinforced through what they say and do (Badaracco and Ellsworth, 1989).

It is apparent that modeling can be important in determining and developing behavior within an organization. Social learning theory provides a framework describing how modeling can be effective in influencing the behavior of individuals.

Social Learning Theory

The name of this theory reveals the emphasis that it places on learning from other individuals (Davis and Luthans, 1980). Exposure to social models accounts to a great extent for how behaviors are transmitted among people, either inadvertently or deliberately (Bandura, 1977a).

As a behavioral theory, social learning theory draws heavily upon the principles of classical and operant conditioning. (Operant conditioning influences behavior through rewards that reinforce the behavior. The person acts in ways to receive the rewards.) In addition, social learning theory acknowledges that learning is also affected by vicarious learning (modeling), covert cognitive processes, and self-control processes (Luthans and Kreitner, 1985).

According to social learning theory, much of our behavior is acquired by observing and then imitating others. It is not, however, a simple case of "monkey see, monkey do." Cognitive factors help influence what behaviors will be observed and how these behaviors will be perceived. Individuals, behaviors, and the environment all interact with and influence one another. In addition, individuals are capable of exercising control over their own behavior (Bandura, 1977b). Because of the attention given to the three processes of vicarious learning, cognition, and self-control, social learning theory is different from operant conditioning (Kreitner and Luthans, 1984).

Albert Bandura is the most widely recognized expert on social learning theory. Bandura (1977b) has strongly emphasized the importance of vicarious learning, or modeling, in his development of social learning theory. Individuals learn vicariously by observing the behavior of other people and the resulting consequences related to their behavior. By learning from observing others, many needless and costly errors can be avoided. Learning would be very laborious if people had to rely on trial and error, with only the results of their own behavior to guide them. When observing others, individuals can develop ideas of how to perform new behaviors and then use the ideas later as guides for their own actions.

Vicarious learning, or modeling, consists of four distinct processes: attentional, retention, motor reproduction, and motivational (Bandura, 1977b). By developing insight into how these complex and interrelated processes work, we can better understand modeling (Sims and Manz, 1982). These processes have numerous implications for leaders.

For individuals to learn through observation, they must attend to the modeled behavior and accurately perceive it. Attentional processes determine what modeled behaviors are observed and what information is extracted from the observation. A number of factors can affect attentional processes. Individuals with whom one has regular contact have great influence because their behaviors are frequently modeled and are thus most likely to be observed. Also, models who have attractive interpersonal qualities are more likely to be observed than those who do not (Bandura, 1977b).

Modeled behaviors are not very influential if people are unable to remember them. Retention processes enable one to retain observations in memory, usually in some symbolic form such as verbal coding or mental imagery. Mental rehearsal or the actual performance of the modeled behavior can also increase retention (Bandura, 1977b).

In the next process, motor reproduction, individuals use the stored symbolic codings to reproduce the modeled behavior. To be successful, the individual must possess the physical or mental ability necessary to perform the behavior (Sims and Manz, 1982).

Motivational processes have to do with the fact that people are more likely to adopt a behavior that results in positive outcomes than a behavior they think will not be rewarded. Therefore it cannot be assumed that people will enact all modeled behaviors; only those that hold some incentive for them will be adopted (Bandura, 1977b).

Each of the above processes is important in determining the successful acquisition of a modeled behavior. If an observer fails to acquire the behavior of a model, it is likely that the failure is related to one or more of the following causes: failure to attend to the relevant behavior, inadequate symbolic coding, failure to retain learned information, lack of physical ability to perform, or lack of motivation (Bandura, 1977b). By considering each of these different processes, a leader can increase the likelihood that a modeled behavior will be incorporated into an employee's performance.

Modeling and Organizational Behavior

Modeling is a process through which employees can learn either desirable or undesirable work behaviors. Learning from modeling is a daily occurrence in organizations, even if the individuals involved are unaware of the modeling processes (Manz and Sims, 1981). According to Davis and Luthans (1980), employees are more likely to interpret job descriptions, policies, and procedures in the workplace by observing others than by following the written word. A manager's behavior could be more important than any procedural directions. "Do as I say, not as I do" is certainly not an appropriate philosophy for leaders who want to have a positive effect on their followers' behavior. It is a challenge to transformational leaders to utilize the modeling process effectively to enhance the performance of their personnel and organizations (Decker, 1986).

Weiss (1977) stated that social learning theory could provide an understanding of the behavior development processes that occur in organizations. In Weiss's study of modeling and its effect on organizational socialization, results indicated that people develop patterns of work behavior by observing certain co-workers and then imitating observed behaviors. People evidently choose the models they observe based on perceptions of the models' success within the organization and their levels of competence.

As noted before, certain characteristics of observed models tend to increase the likelihood that others will imitate their behaviors. Models who are perceived as being successful and credible, interpersonally attractive, and possessing high status and competence are more likely to have a greater influence on observers. Being too competent, however, can pose a problem. Models who are perceived to possess much greater abilities than the observer may be too threatening to be effective. Apparently observers can sometimes identify more closely with a model who struggles with a problem and is successful than with one who displays no difficulties (Bandura, 1977a; Manz and Sims, 1981).

It is possible that certain characteristics of the observer may also affect the modeling process. However, there has been little research to determine how personal characteristics can influence vicarious learning (Manz and Sims, 1981). Weiss (1977) found that the level of subordinate self-esteem may affect the results of a supervisor's behavioral modeling. Individuals with low self-esteem may be more prone to the influence of modeling. Weiss (1977) also noted that the value the observer places on the consequences of the modeled behavior influences whether or not the behavior will be adopted. If the consequences are not valued, it is less likely that the modeled behavior will be adopted.

Because of his or her position occupied within the organization, a transformational leader is perceived by employees as a model of behavior considered acceptable and desirable within the organization. Therefore it is important that leaders should be keenly aware of what values and behaviors they want to transmit to their employees. To do this successfully, the leader must possess self-understanding and a consistent set of goals, attitudes, and values that guide his or her activities (Brown, 1973). The leader who clearly understands the values or behaviors necessary to facilitate the successful achievement of organizational goals is more likely to be an effective model for employees. Peters and Austin (1985) suggested that leaders should be so unflaggingly consistent in their actions that they could be called "broken records." That type of faithful consistency clearly communicates to employees what is expected of them. When people know what their leaders and organization represent, they can make decisions resulting in the achievement of the organization's goals. This is truly a form of empowerment for employees.

Application of Social Learning Theory

According to Manz and Sims (1981), essentially two types of modeling can serve as sources of learning within organizations. The first and best-known type of modeling is training. Training is typically used in organizations to introduce new skills or behaviors. The second type of modeling, which is very important but not as well known, is that which occurs on a daily basis between managers and employees. In this type of modeling, the manager either intentionally or unintentionally serves as a model for employee behavior. Learning occurs through the employee's daily observations of the manager's behaviors. Because of the status, prestige, and level of experience usually associated with a managerial position, employees are more inclined to imitate a manager's behavior than a co-worker's behavior. In addition, managers can influence behavior because of their ability to reward. When a manager seeks to reward an employee in a manner that is apparent to other employees, the manager is developing an effective model to guide the future behavior of other employees.

In training programs essentially four stages are necessary for effective modeling to take place: (1) modeling of desired behavior; (2) behavioral rehearsal; (3) social reinforcement; and (4) transfer of training. These stages are closely related to the four modeling processes identified by Bandura (1977b), that were discussed previously.

In the first phase, the modeling of the desired behavior, the basis for the change is established and models are presented. These models may be live or may be on film or videotape. This stage is closely associated with the factors that influence the attentional processes (Manz and Sims, 1981). Accordingly, steps must be taken to facilitate attention to the model. First, the model should be someone of credibility or high status; this is why the leader is an appropriate model. Second, the behavior should be modeled in a positive, favorable environment at a level appropriate to the observer's capability. Third, demonstration of the modeled behavior should be repeated for the observer several times. And finally, the behavior should be demonstrated in a detailed manner with the positive consequences of the modeled behavior clearly identified (Decker, 1986; Sims and Manz, 1982).

The second training phase is rehearsal of the behavior. This stage, associated with the retention processes of modeling, takes place when observers practice the behaviors that have been modeled. For learning to be enhanced, it is important that the observers be given an opportunity to practice the behaviors that have been demonstrated. Retention will be increased if the observer is encouraged to rehearse the behavior mentally and act it out in the training environment (Decker, 1986; Manz and Sims, 1981; Sims and Manz, 1982).

The third phase is social reinforcement, during which positive feedback is provided to trainees to reinforce the desired behaviors as they are produced. This reinforcement is designed to motivate the trainees to continue the desired behavior. This phase relates to Bandura's (1977b) motivational processes (Manz and Sims, 1981; Sims and Manz, 1982).

The final phase in training is the transfer of newly acquired skills into the "real" work world. This phase is associated with the motor reproduction processes of modeling. Sims and Manz (1982) stated that difficulty with the transfer of training from the practice setting into the work setting is probably the major reason why training efforts fail. However, the manager can initiate a number of actions to help facilitate this transfer of training. Some examples include the following: (1) accurate identification of problem situations before beginning the training program; (2) provision of individualized reinforcement and follow-up; and (3) post-training group meetings that allow participants to discuss application problems and to rehearse any proposed solutions to these problems (Manz and Sims, 1981). It is important to remember that behaviors learned in the sheltered environment of a training session must be reinforced in the actual work environment if they are to be successfully transferred.

Compared to training, the modeling that occurs on a daily basis between leaders and employees is a more subtle form of modeling. However, it is no less important as a means of socializing employees into the organizational culture. Managers are very visible and important role models to their employees. The behaviors that leaders display serve as guides for the behavior of other employees. For example, by exhibiting such characteristics as sensitivity, tact, and cooperation when interacting with other employees, the leader clearly demonstrates behaviors considered acceptable in interpersonal relations within the organization. On the other hand, leaders who espouse certain values but whose actions indicate otherwise will lose credibility with their employees. Such "do as I say, not as I do" leaders would do well to heed the truth in the Native American saying, "What you do speaks so loudly that I cannot hear what you say" (Kreitner and Luthans, 1984).

Research Implications of Social Learning Theory

Much of the research published about the effects of vicarious learning, or modeling, has supported its effectiveness in training situations (Manz and Sims, 1981). Decker (1986) stated that although a social learning theory approach to leadership has been theoretically developed, research and application of this leadership approach has just begun. The research to date has focused primarily on the effectiveness of modeling when used to teach psychomotor and social skills, while cognitive skills have not received as much emphasis. Cognitive modeling does occur, but not in an overt, observable manner. Models who are teaching cognitive skills must make their covert mental processes understood by explaining to their observers each mental step in the decision process to their observers. The effectiveness of cognitive modeling needs to be documented more thoroughly in the research literature.

Through research it has been determined that modeling is not the simple, imitative process it was first thought to be. Weiss (1977) studied the impact of specific social characteristics on the effectiveness of behavior modeling. The results indicated that workers were more likely to imitate their supervisor's behavior if they perceived the supervisor to be competent and successful within the organization. However, it was also determined that behavioral similarity was not necessarily related to the subordinate's perception of the supervisor's reward power. Subordinates evidently differed in how much they valued the expected reward outcome. Weiss (1977) stated that the results suggested there are cognitive motivational factors that intervene to affect the socializing environment and behavior change relationship.

Manz and Sims's (1986) research supported the contention that modeling is a considerably complex process consisting of multiple affective and behavioral linkages. Manz and Sims (1986) investigated the effect of a modeling stimulus (observing a model leader's behavior) on the subsequent behavior of the observers, hypothesizing that the observers would respond by imitating the modeled behavior. However, this did not happen. Direct, imitative changes did occur in some situations, although unexpected indirect changes were also noted in other instances. One explanation of the results could be that the observers cognitively evaluated the model, thus leading to different behavioral outcomes. Manz and Sims (1986) stated that there appears to be a need for more research to explore the effect of modeling processes on the observer's subsequent behavior and responses.

Gioia and Manz (1985) stated that because vicarious learning and modeling are such important organizational behavioral processes it is essential to explore the cognitive mechanisms by which they work. Vicarious learning can be described simply as "the observation of a model and the retention of the observed behavior as a guide to appropriate action in a specific situation" (Gioia and Manz, 1985, p. 531). When vicarious learning occurs, the observer is learning a behavioral script from the model. These scripts, which are then held in the memory of the observer, serve as a basis from which understanding and behavior develop. When the appropriate situational cues are present, these cognitive scripts guide the enactment of the performative script, which is the observer's own performance of the previously modeled behaviors. The ability to change an observer's behavior through modeling is dependent upon the effective teaching of these cognitive scripts, or the effective alteration of previously held cognitive scripts. Gioia and Manz (1985) urged further investigation into this "bridge" between cognition and behavior to provide a useful perspective for management practice and research.

Because social learning theory examines behavioral and cognitive processes in the environment in which they occur, certain implications for research must be considered. Most notably, to rely only upon questionnaires to measure behavior is inadequate in a social learning approach. More effort must be made to directly observe the behavior in its interactive elements, in the "real" world. To establish social learning theory as an appropriate base from which to study organizational behavior, research should be conducted to examine the dynamics among persons, behaviors, and environment (Davis and Luthans, 1980).

☐ *Implications for Nursing*

The role of a nurse executive is dynamic and multi-faceted. Nurse executives and leaders in educational and practice settings have unique opportunities to influence and even create the environment in which professional nursing practice can flourish. In this highly influential role, the nurse leader has a major responsibility for changing the behavior in an organization to provide an environment supportive of the preparation and retention of competent and expert practitioners (Pfoutz, Simms and Price, 1987). It is part of the nurse leader's role to serve as a model in providing effective socialization experiences that impart the appropriate values, beliefs, behaviors, and skills to individuals within their organizations.

□ Application to Nursing: Case Study

The nursing manager of a 500-bed hospital has been concerned about the particularly high turnover rate of registered nurses on one of her general medical-surgical nursing floors. A study of the RN turnover rate on this unit revealed that it is higher than other units within the hospital, with the average length of employment for newly hired RNs ranging from 6 to 12 months. This has affected the staff's ability to provide high quality patient care consistently.

Data gathered from exit interviews with RNs leaving the unit show the most frequently cited reasons for leaving to be: (1) a lack of clearly defined expectations for the RN on the part of unit management; (2) a lack of peer support or guidance displayed by the more senior, experienced RNs; (3) an inadequate orientation to the unit, both in content and length of time; and (4) a perceived lack of opportunity to pursue individual professional development goals.

The nursing manager has hired a new unit manager for the unit. One of the unit manager's first priorities is to decrease the amount of turnover among the RNs and to increase the level of job satisfaction on the unit. She has decided to accomplish these goals by first addressing the concerns most frequently cited by the RNs who have left the unit.

Questions for Discussion

1. Based upon the information you have, what conclusions might you draw about the socialization process currently in place on this unit?
2. How can social learning theory be applied to this situation?
3. What would the unit manager's role be in applying social learning theory to this situation?
4. What characteristics would the unit manager need to possess and demonstrate in order to be successfully identified as a role model for the staff?
5. Select one of the four unit problems identified in the case study. From the perspective of the unit manager, use social learning theory as a framework to outline an intervention plan for resolving the problem.

References

Badaracco, J. L. and Ellsworth, R.R. (1989). *Leadership and the quest for integrity.* Boston: Harvard Business School Press.

Bandura, A. (1977a). Analysis of modeling processes. In Clarizio, H.F., Craig, R.C., and Mehrens, W.A. editors: *Contemporary issues in educational psychology* (pp. 123-126). Boston: Allyn-Bacon.

Bandura, A. (1977b). *Social learning theory.* Englewood Cliffs, N.J.: Prentice-Hall.

Bennis, W. and Nanus, B. (1985). *Leaders.* New York: Harper & Row.

Brown, J. D. (1973). *The human nature of organizations.* New York: AMACOM.

Davis, T. and Luthans, F. (1980). A social learning approach to organizational behavior. *Academy of Management Review, 5*(2), 281-290.

Decker, P. J. (1986). Social learning theory and leadership. *Journal of Management Development, 5*(3), 46-58.

Gardner, J.W. (1986). *The heart of the matter: leader-constituent interaction.* (Leadership Papers/3 — Leadership Studies Program). Washington, D.C.: Independent Sector.

Gibson, J., Ivancevich, J., and Donnelly, J. (1982). *Organizations: behavior, structure, processes.* Plano, Tex.: Business Publications.

Gioia, D. and Manz, C. (1985). Linking cognition and behavior: a script processing interpretation of vicarious learning. *Academy of Management Review, 10*(3), 527-539.

Kreitner, R. and Luthans, F. (1984). A social learning approach to behavioral management: Radical behaviorists "mellowing out". *Organizational Dynamics, 13*(2), 47-65.

Louis, M. R. (1980). Surprise and sense making: What newcomers experience in entering unfamiliar organizational settings. *Administrative Science Quarterly, 25*(2), 226-248.

Luthans, F. and Kreitner, R. (1985). *Organizational behavior modification and beyond.* Glenview, Ill: Scott, Foresman, and Company.

Manz, C. and Sims, H. (1981). Vicarious learning: the influence of modeling on organizational behavior. *Academy of Management Review, 6*(1), 105-113.

Manz, C. and Sims, H. (1986). Beyond imitation: complex behavioral and affective linkages resulting from exposure to leadership training models. *Journal of Applied Psychology, 71*(4), 571-578.

Peters, T. and Austin, N. (1985). *A passion for excellence: the leadership difference.* New York: Random House.

Pfeffer, J. (1982). *Organizations and organization theory.* Cambridge, Mass: Ballinger Publishing.

Pfoutz, S., Simms, L., and Price, S. (1987). Teaching and learning: essential components of the nurse executive role. *Image: Journal of Nursing Scholarship, 19*(3), 138-141.

Sims, H. and Manz, C. (1982). Modeling influences on employee behavior. *Personnel Journal, 61*(1), 58-65.

Weiss, H. (1977). Subordinate imitation of supervisor behavior: The role of modeling in organizational socialization. *Organizational Behavior and Human Performance, 19*(1), 89-105.

9

NANCY L. DILLARD

Development of Hardiness

CHAPTER OBJECTIVES

- □ List three components of hardiness.
- □ Describe five ways a nursing leader can demonstrate hardiness.
- □ Describe benefits of hardiness in nursing leaders.
- □ Explain benefits of hardiness in followers.
- □ Compare and contrast the effects of two leadership styles upon development of hardiness among followers.
- □ Evaluate hardiness characteristics in self.

L eadership can be defined as the ability to influence people to work to meet certain goals. Effective leadership involves one's ability to adapt leadership styles to meet organizational goals and needs as environmental changes occur. Leadership affects all levels of organization, and leadership behaviors affect followers (Hall, 1988; Tucker, 1984; Birnbaum, 1988; Hershey and Blanchard, 1982).

Hardiness is a personality characteristic that can enable and empower a leader to withstand and adapt to change and stress. Hardiness, or resilience, is composed of control, commitment, and challenge. Hardiness has been studied for several years in terms of adaptation of seeds and plants to the environment. Resilience and hardiness also apply to leadership in relation to the leader's response to stressful events and adaptation to environmental change. Hardiness denotes leadership strength in a variety of situations and is a trait that would benefit followers.

Hardiness

Numerous authors* have studied personality hardiness among leaders with respect to stressful life events and health. Control, the first component of hardiness, relates to internal-external locus of control. Hardy leaders believe that they have control or influence over events in their lives (internal locus of control), in contrast with persons who feel powerless in various situations (external locus of control). The sense of control and recognition of choices in situations provide empowerment as the leader makes decisions and plans for the organizational structure. Lack of hardiness is demonstrated by feelings of powerlessness in most situations, as when a person feels controlled by other persons, environmental conditions, or change.

Hardy leaders are also committed leaders. Commitment is defined as the ability to feel deeply involved in life activities; an example is one's commitment to family or work. A leader who is committed to specific life activities is not threatened when environmental conditions change. Leaders demonstrate flexibility and endurance as they meet organizational changes with a strong

---

* Kobasa (1979), Kobasa, Maddi, and Courington (1981), Kobasa, Maddi, and Kahn (1982), and Kobasa and Maddi (1984)

commitment to self and to work. They develop clearly defined goals and values as they recognize their capabilities to work in new situations with new subordinates or supervisors, to learn new job skills, and to cope with change. They learn from new experiences and events, with a perspective of self-growth, not alienation. When leaders are committed to the organization, followers are also likely to be committed. Leaders who lack commitment are frequently bored and lonely and they lack a sense of purpose. If leaders model negative behaviors, lack of productivity and organizational stagnation are likely to follow.

Finally, hardy leaders face new situations and change with increased energy because they view change as a challenge, not a threat. Change is viewed as a way of life and an opportunity for growth. Recognizing that an organization is an open system that interacts with and adapts to environmental changes, the leader anticipates and guides the organization through change. The leader is also willing to envision future needs of the organization and take risks in making innovative changes so that the organization can grow, become better and more efficient, and develop new capabilities. Too much change and challenge can be frightening for leaders and followers. Factors that can increase leader hardiness include looking at change as something to be expected, seeing work or new work as a challenge, and being committed to self and to work.

A leader does not single-handedly achieve success in an organization. Leaders involve their followers in the change process by giving direction, modeling needed behaviors, and enabling the followers to act. Leaders who demonstrate hardiness also demonstrate power. By modeling the positive aspects of control, commitment, and challenge, leaders can foster development of hardiness in their followers. This encourages growth among the followers and within the organization (Kouzes and Posner, 1987).

Characteristics basic to an effective and hardy leader include coherence and consistency in beliefs and values, in daily work behavior, and in organizational goals. Strong personal ethics — primarily honesty and fairness — are fundamental to the leader to enhance follower trust and honesty. Leaders must have a strong belief in others to provide empowerment to followers. Followers are frequently interested in self-enhancement, and leaders can foster organizational growth by enabling followers to work in specific organizational areas that benefit both the individual and the group.

The transformational leader must clearly convey organizational goals to followers and enable followers to see how individual roles contribute to organizational functions and visionary aims. The transformational leader conveys to others that organizational aims and standards will be high, not mediocre. Followers will be told they were chosen for their knowledge and skills, and they can handle their tasks and have the potential to excel. The leader actively recruits workers with strengths that will make outstanding contributions to company goals. The leader also works with followers to help them develop higher level skills and abilities.

A leader maintains open communication with employees about problems, aims, and quality of work. Autonomy is encouraged and fostered so that individuals will feel a sense of ownership for the organization and will increase commitment. If employee commitment is high, tasks are likely to be completed faster, more thoroughly, and more efficiently.

In summary, important leadership characteristics for an effective leader, include honesty, trust, integrity, open communication, high ethical standards, and flexibility. Additional traits include willingness to take risks, to be supportive and encouraging to workers for growth and autonomy, and to recognize achievement (Badaracco and Ellsworth, 1989; Bennis, 1959; Bennis and Nanus, 1985). When problems arise, the leader may need to clarify and restate organizational aims to decrease ambiguity. The leader can enhance hardiness in followers by modeling how to handle confrontation. Confrontation must be confined to the issue in question and must not expand into personality issues. Demonstrating a willingness to listen to workers' explanations of a problem will result in enhanced worker respect for the leader and will enable the leader to understand the area of conflict. Badaracco and Ellsworth (1989) caution against the use of negotiation and compromise in handling areas of conflict because compromise can lead to a lowering of company goals and standards. Compromise can also lead to workers' beliefs that management is not committed to organizational goals. Rather than altering organizational aims, the leader should assist followers in identifying existing problems and in decision-making strategies and actions to resolve the problems. The leader's ability to enable workers to settle their differences without altering company goals can foster open communication, respect for others, courage to grow, and greater commitment to the organization.

Developing Hardiness in Followers

Characteristics of followers are similar to those of the leader. They include honesty, competence, enthusiasm, direction, and a positive attitude. When these characteristics are present, followers are more likely to have pride in the organization, to see consistency between the organizational values and their own, and to feel as if they have influence in the organization. When the desired characteristics are not found in the employees, the leader must continue to model the expected behaviors and provide encouragement as followers work to develop these strengths.

The leader can foster development of control in followers by encouraging them to recognize choices that are available, to make choices, and to accept responsibility and accountability for the choices. Followers should be assisted in evaluating their own responses to situations and stresses. If followers lack the skills or knowledge to cope with or adapt to specific situations, the leader can encourage the followers to attend workshops or seminars or to work with other followers who have strengths in those areas. Goals for the followers can be set and their achievement can be measured; this will strengthen followers' recognition of the effects of their choices. By modeling control and enabling followers to develop a sense of control, the leader fosters growth toward hardiness in followers.

Another component of hardiness is commitment. Development of commitment to self is as important as development of commitment to work. The leader can assist followers in setting specific, realistic, and attainable goals for personal growth and work. Organizational goals can be discussed and explained in meetings and forums set up to help employees understand the rationale for any specific changes. The leader also has some control by rewarding employees for work commitment and goal attainment through salary changes, merit pay, and bonuses. Thus, commitment to self and work can be modeled and fostered by the leader.

Enabling the follower to view work and change as challenge instead of threat is one of the most difficult tasks facing the leader. The leader can assess followers' strengths related to job function and task requirements. If a job matches the follower's desired area of work, or niche, then the employee is more likely to be committed to the work and to see the job as a challenge, not a threat. Kouzes and Posner (1987) suggest that to be effective, the leader must find opportunities for followers to explore, discover, solve problems, and determine how to deal with external threats. The leader must know the strengths of individual followers in order to provide a balance between challenging and routine activities, thus enabling them to perform well within their capabilities.

Leadership Styles and Follower Hardiness

Leadership styles will affect development of hardiness in followers. Charismatic leaders depend heavily on emotional appeal and control of followers. They expect followers to conform to their standards and their values. Leaders have a message to give to followers, and followers can decide whether they will follow the leader. If followers are committed to the leader, then commitment to work will continue as long as the work relates to the leader's goals and desires. The leader's control depends on the follower's perception of uncertainty within the environment. If followers perceive a great amount of uncertainty in their surroundings, then their commitment and responses to the leader will be more intense than if they felt only minimal uncertainty. Followers of charismatic leaders are less likely to be empowered by the leader to develop hardiness because the leader thrives on their dependence. However, the leader is likely to demonstrate hardiness by control, commitment to beliefs and work, and a view of visionary goals as a challenge (Avolio and Bass, 1988).

Transformational leaders are likely to model hardiness and also to develop hardiness in their followers. The transformational leader attends to the follower's needs, treating the follower with respect as an individual. This kind of leader works to increase followers' self-esteem and self-confidence, modeling empowerment to those who feel powerless. The transformational leader also models internal locus of control and views work as a major life interest, accepting challenge readily and identifying a goal as a task to be performed by the group. The leader motivates followers to work toward specific goals, not self-interest. Followers of the transformational leader are encouraged to be independent, make their own decisions, and see change as a challenge that will increase work levels (Avolio and Bass, 1988; Byrd, 1987).

Self-assessment of personality style can enable the leader to identify his or her own decision-making strengths and to determine what type of information must be obtained from others before final decisions can be made. Knowledge of personality types of followers can assist the leader in determining task assignments and in fostering teamwork within a work group. The leader will work to achieve a balance between introverts and extroverts, sensing and intuitive types, judging and perceptive types, and thinking and feeling types. The balance of personality types in work groups will be more effective as the leader encourages and emphasizes strengths of each member, minimizing individual weaknesses (Fruend, 1989).

Organizational Culture

Coeling and Wilcox (1988), del Bueno and Vincent (1986), and Saffold (1988) describe the importance of culture in an organization. Organizational culture is comprised of group norms and values and is reflected in the group's communication, decision-making, manner of dress, behavior, and adaptation to change. Two areas of culture are important for the leader to understand. First, the leader must be aware that adding a new member to a functioning work group can be detrimental to both the group and the member if cultural "fit" is not attempted. For example, if a group is extremely autocratic and follows policies for all decisions, a new member who is used to participative leadership will become frustrated by the structure of the group. Employees who do not fit the mold may seek to change jobs.

The leader's responsibility in promoting hardiness in new employees begins with identifying potential workers who will fit within the subunit's culture. The leader assesses characteristics of the subunit's dress, behavior, communication, and power structure. When job interviews are conducted, the leader should look for an employee who will not only fit the job description but also work well within the subunit culture. During orientation, the leader and group members will help the new worker identify specific work strategies, decision-making models, and group values. Such orientation will help the worker focus on the job as a challenge and will enable her to see the levels of control that she and the group exercise within the work environment.

Understanding organizational culture is also important for the leader when organizational changes occur. The leader can help followers identify needed changes and how the changes can be made within each subunit. The leader will know where to expect resistance within the group as well as what kind of resistance it will be. Prior knowledge of the subunit's functioning will assist the leader in knowing when and how to introduce the change so that resistance can be decreased.

The leader must also be aware that when major changes are made in organizational culture the addition of a single new member who is agreeable to the change will not in itself lead to successful change. Change is successful only when a new work group, prepared to incorporate the needed change, begins to work with the older group. The hard work of change remains. The use of knowledge of organizational culture in the leader's planning and implementation of change will also decrease costs of hiring and rehiring. Thus the hardy leader must know the process of change and must develop strategies for change based on organizational values and practices.

Leadership characteristics are expected to be somewhat different in the future. Byrd (1987), Thomas (1988), and Cameron and Whetten (1981) suggested leadership characteristics for changing environments. Leaders working within open systems must adapt to environmental changes by being visionary or being committed to a vision. Anticipatory skills include the leader's insight into the changing environment as well as the ability to provide new services and develop new agency strengths.

Networking within organizations serves to promote open communication, gather information across work groups, recognize changes in goals, foster discussion of economic trends and political changes, and encourage exchange of ideas as the organization grows. Yukl (1989) and Nelson (1989) identify advantages of development and use of social networks for use in decision-making and in handling conflict within or between groups. However, the leader must be aware of the potential for competition and increased conflict between groups if networking is not well-planned and organized. Networking is also identified as a method to review personnel or look for changes in personnel within the organization.

Commitment toward self and work must be developed within each individual. The leader also focuses on empowering followers to be independent, to grow, to enhance individual strengths, and to develop skills. Use of a peer support group has been identified as a strategy that can be helpful in enhancing hardiness and providing encouragement to everyone, from the new member of a work group to the leader (Zins, Murphy, Maher, and Wess, 1988).

Finally, Henry and LeClair (1987) described the importance of language in strengthening leadership. Empowerment of the leader is enhanced by effective communication skills and the use of proper words. Therefore, the leader must develop a vocabulary in "leadership language" and support followers, giving rationale for specific actions and helping the followers develop into hardy workers.

❑ Implications for Nursing

The characteristic of hardiness will enhance nursing leadership's effectiveness in healthy adaptation to environmental changes. Behaviors of hardiness found in the nursing leader include a strong sense of commitment to work and to self; a sense of control over current job responsibilities and situations that arise; and the ability to face each change as a challenge, rather than feeling threatened, alienated, or externally controlled. As nursing leaders model hardy behaviors and enable followers to develop hardiness, work will become more efficient and productive. Organizational changes, which are inevitable, will seem less threatening, and workers will feel more committed and have a sense of ownership within the organization.

❑ Application to Nursing: Case Study

A nurse was caring for Tom Marsh, a 68-year-old man with Alzheimer's disease who lives with his wife, Susan. When the nurse visited the home to evaluate Mr. Marsh, Susan said that she was having a great deal of difficulty with her husband. As the nurse explored the problem, she learned that Susan had not had a day out with friends for the previous 3 months. Their children rarely visited because they are embarrassed by their father's behavior. Susan said she was under a great deal of stress and needed help. She went on to say that the doctor's response was to suggest placing her husband in a nursing home, but Susan was not prepared to do this. She wanted to continue caring for him at home.

The nurse recognized that Alzheimer's patients are very difficult to care for and that caregivers undergo stress, frustration, and even depression. The situation was discussed at length, and Susan concluded that she really wanted to continue caring for her husband at home.

Susan was like many other people who care for Alzheimer's patients and faced the same types of problems: a change in social support, stress and frustration, and depression (Robinson, 1989). High level hardiness is a valuable asset to a caregiver in this situation. The nurse analyzed the situation and recognized that Susan was providing excellent physical care for her husband but that she needed help coping. Susan was beginning to feel powerless in her current situation, but she was committed to her husband and to his care. To help her increase control in the situation, options were reviewed. Because her finances would have enabled her to pay for assistance, one idea involved hiring a home health aide to assist in Mr. Marsh's care during the evening; this would help Susan get more sleep. A local adult day care center was willing to provide care for Tom during the day, allowing Susan to get out of the house and socialize with friends. Susan was also encouraged to get involved in the local Alzheimer's support group. Susan recognized that there might be a time when she would be unable to care for her husband at home. Susan's "letting go" of her husband would be a painful experience, but she would have increased support from families who have had similar circumstances. She also decided to see a counselor who worked with caregivers.

The nurse helped Susan mobilize her resources and identify choices she had in her difficult situation. These things helped her achieve more hardiness. The nurse explained choices regarding her husband's care, spent time listening to her, and explored her feelings of frustration and powerlessness as well as her fears of placing Tom in a nursing home. The nurse was also aware of Susan's decreased care of herself. Susan had to learn to monitor her own health so she would know when she needed assistance. She needed to enjoy time once again with family and friends and to increase her commitment to self.

Hardiness can be increased by working to decrease feelings of powerlessness. In this instance Susan needed to talk about her feelings and seek assistance in reviewing options. If she was able to choose the kinds of assistance for her husband and herself she would feel more in control of the situation. Obtaining assistance in the overall care of her husband would enable her to increase her activities with other family members and friends.

The nurse provided leadership in development of hardiness of individual caregivers, as well as in other health care workers. Hardiness enhanced coping in stressful situations.

Questions for Discussion

1. How can a nurse appraise the hardiness of a caregiver?
2. In this case, did Susan interpret her husband's illness as a challenge or as a threat? Give the rationale for your answer.

3. How can caregivers regain control of their situations?
4. What interventions can be used to increase commitment to self?

References

Avolio, B.J. and Bass, B.M. (1988). Transformational leadership, charisma, and beyond. In Hunt, J. G., Baliga, B.R., Dachler, H.P., and Schreischeim, C.A., editors: *Emerging leadership vistas* (pp. 29-49). Lexington, Mass.: Lexington Books.

Badaracco, J.L. and Ellsworth, R.R. (1989). *Leadership and the quest for integrity.* Boston: Harvard Business School.

Bennis, W.G. (1959). Leadership theory and administrative behavior: the problem of authority. *Administrative Science Quarterly, 4*(3), 259-301.

Bennis, W.G. and Nanus, B. (1985). *Leadership: the strategies for taking charge.* San Francisco: Harper & Row.

Birnbaum, R. (1988). *How colleges work.* San Francisco: Jossey-Bass.

Byrd, R.E. (1987). Corporate leadership skills: a new synthesis. *Organizational Dynamics, 16*(1), 34-43.

Cameron, K.S. and Whetten, D.A. (1981). Perceptions of organizational life cycles. *Administrative Science Quarterly, 25*(4), 525-544.

Coeling, H.V. and Wilcox, J.R. (1988). Understanding organizational culture: a key to management decision-making. *Journal of Nursing Administration, 18*(11), 16-24.

del Bueno, D.J. and Vincent, P.M. (1986). Organizational culture: How important is it? *Journal of Nursing Administration, 16*(10), 15-20.

Fruend, C. (1989). Assessing decision-making style with type theory. In Henry, B., Arndt, C., De Vincenti, M., and Marriner-Tomey, A., editors, *Dimensions of Nursing Administration* (pp. 427-453). Boston: Blackwell Scientific Publications.

Hall, R.H. (1988). *Organizations: structure and process* (ed. 5). Englewood Cliffs, N.J.: Prentice Hall.

Henry, B. and LeClair, H. (1987). Language, leadership, and power. *Journal of Nursing Administration, 17*(1), 19-25.

Hershey, P. and Blanchard, K. (1982). *Management of organizational behavior* (ed. 4). Englewood Cliffs, N.J.: Prentice Hall.

Kobasa, S.C. (1979). Stressful life events, personality, and health: an inquiry into hardiness. *Journal of Personality and Social Psychology, 37*(1), 1-11.

Kobasa, S.C. and Maddi, S.R. (1984). *The hardy executive: health under stress.* Homewood, Ill.: Dow Jones-Irwin.

Kobasa, S.C., Maddi, S.R., and Courington, S. (1981). Personality and constitution as mediators in the stress-illness relationship. *Journal of Health and Social Behavior, 22*(12), 368-378.

Kobasa, S.C., Maddi, S.R. and Kahn, S. (1982). Hardiness and health: a prospective study. *Journal of Personality and Social Psychology, 42*(3), 168-177.

Kouzes, J.M. and Posner, B.Z. (1987). *The leadership challenge.* San Francisco: Jossey-Bass.

Nelson, R.E. (1989). The strength of strong ties: social networks and inter group conflict in organizations. *Academy of Management Journal, 32*(2), 377-401.

Robinson, K.L. (1989). Predictors of depression among wife care-givers. *Nursing Research, 38*(6), 359-363.

Saffold, G.S. (1988). Culture traits, strength, and organizational performance: moving beyond "strong" culture. *Academy of Management Review, 13*(4), 546-558.

Thomas, A.B. (1988). Does leadership make a difference to organizational performance? *Administrative Science Quarterly, 33*(3), 388-400.

Tucker, A. (1984). *Chairing the academic department* (ed. 2). New York: Collier Macmillan.

Yukl, G.A. (1989). *Leadership in organizations* (ed. 2). Englewood Cliffs, N.J.: Prentice Hall.

Zins, J.E., Murphy, J.J., Maher, C.A., and Wess, B.P. (1988). The peer support group: a means to facilitate professional development. *School Psychology Review, 17*(1), 138-146.

V

Empowerment

10

JUDITH W. ALEXANDER

Technology for Leadership

CHAPTER OBJECTIVES

- ☐ Identify the meaning of technology for nursing.
- ☐ Discuss theoretical perspectives in the development of technology for leadership.
- ☐ Explain the nature of technology in empowering nursing leaders to achieve goals.
- ☐ Describe the appropriate match of technology and leadership style for the transformational leader.
- ☐ Analyze the technology-leadership match at work group (unit), organizational, and boundary-spanning levels.
- ☐ Demonstrate how technology and leadership can be used to improve quality, access, and cost outcomes in nursing.

M uch has been written about using contingency (situational) theory to explain the behavior of organizations and how factors of importance to organizations can best be matched to improve effectiveness and efficiency (Child, 1972; Mark, 1989; Perrow, 1967; Woodward, 1965). Leavitt (1965) viewed organizations as dependent upon at least four interacting variables: task, human, structure, and technology. Much later, Peters and Austin (1985) spelled out how leadership is the element needed to connect these interacting variables. This chapter focuses on how the technology of the nursing leader's work environment can be used to empower nurses in selecting the appropriate leadership direction.

Technology

Technology is the action performed on an input to produce an output. Basic material is taken into the organization, certain actions are performed on that material, and the material is altered in the desired fashion (Perrow, 1967). The study of technology in organizational analysis involves much more than the machinery or equipment used to produce the goods or services (Hall, 1991). In health care institutions the technology is a set of procedures aimed at changing the physical, psychological, social, or cultural attributes of people from a given status, usually illness, to a new prescribed status, usually wellness (Hasenfeld, 1983).

Technology may be studied at the individual, group (unit), and organizational levels. However, most research shows that characteristics of technology at one level often are not reflected in the organization's technology at the next level (Fry and Slocum, 1984; Ito and Peterson, 1986). In this chapter, technology is discussed at the work group (unit) level because that is the level at which leadership has the greatest impact. The unit is viewed as the people who interact to accomplish the goals of the group. Additionally, Hall (1991) states that regardless of the level within the organization, the situation that is faced and the personnel who are involved (the work group) determine the most effective leadership form.

Within health care institutions, several theoretical descriptions of technology have been presented. Perrow (1967) developed a classification of technology based on the perceived nature of raw materials upon which technological actions are to be performed and on the variability of the raw materials. These aspects of technology produce a 2 × 2 matrix whose dimensions are task predictability (based on the number of exceptional cases that occur in the work); and problem analyzability (described as the nature of the decision making process undertaken when exceptions occur). In another article, Perrow (1965) showed that hospitals appear to fall in several of the four boxes of the matrix, depending upon the nature of the department or unit within the hospital being examined. For example, an emergency room would be in the box representing unstable task predictability and a low understanding of task analyzability. However, a postpartum unit would have stable task predictability and well-understood task analyzability.

Overton, Schneck, and Hazlett (1977) developed a model for nursing units to classify the routineness of technology. The three aspects of work studied by these authors were the nature of the patients being cared for, the techniques employed to care for patients, and the degree of interdependence among the nurses carrying out patient care. The resulting dimensions were labeled instability, variability, and uncertainty. Instability refers to unpredictable fluctuations in patients and techniques. Variability represents differences among patients. Uncertainty expresses the degree to which patients are not well-understood. Using this model, Overton et al. (1977) found that different nursing units have different technologies. For example, psychiatric units were found to be high in uncertainty and variability while being low in instability; intensive care units were found to be high in uncertainty and instability but low in variability.

Verran and Reid (1987) presented a Nursing Technology Model for ambulatory settings. This model was based on Perrow's (1967) work and measured task predictability by the constructs "Standardized Treatment" and "Workflow Variability." Problem analyzability was measured with the constructs "Knowledge of Client" and "Analysis of Intervention Strategies." The results were presented as relationships between the constructs. The authors did not attempt to present the variations of technologies across types of ambulatory settings.

These classifications of technology demonstrate that technology provides a useful way to describe the work activities of nursing organizations (Alexander and Mark, 1990). The discussion so far has focused on internal technologies of organizations. However, research has shown that although technology is implemented at the unit level, changes in technology usually result from the interaction between the organization and the environment (Lawrence and Lorsch, 1967). Organizations operating in uncertain and dynamic environments conduct business differently than do those operating in rather certain and unchanging technological environments. Changes within the environment are introduced to the organization through new personnel, new clients, or current personnel practicing boundary-spanning activities. These individuals have contact with alternative technologies and advocate their use in the organization.

Thus technology becomes an empowering variable whether the leader is dealing with internal or external technologies.

Leadership

Much has been written on leadership and leadership styles. A brief discussion is presented here to establish the relationship between technology and leadership. Leadership is the "ability, based on the personal qualities of the leader, to elicit the followers' voluntary compliance in a broad range of matters" (Etzioni, 1965, p. 690).

Yukl (1981) provided an overview of leadership patterns that indicates how leadership traits and skills affect behaviors and power. These traits and skills in turn interact with exogenous situational (i.e., external to the immediate situation) and intervening variables and contribute to end-result variables of group performance and goal attainment. Technology is one of the exogenous situational variables.

Much of the writing on leadership has focused on the two contrasting approaches to the leadership role: the authoritarian, task-oriented approach versus the supportive, socioemotional approach. These writings show that the appropriate leadership style depends on the situation (a contingency approach). In stable, structured situations, a stricter, more autocratic style of leadership is most likely to be successful. In a situation of change, external threat, and ambiguity, the more lenient, participative style is most effective (Fiedler, 1967, 1972). Technology is one of the determinants of the stability of the organizational situation. Technological factors set limits on the amount and kinds of variations that can be introduced into the organization, thus limiting what the leader can do (Hall, 1991).

Applications of Technology for Leadership in Nursing Care

Application of the technology contingency (determinant) to the leadership direction of the organization can be accomplished at several levels: at the unit level, where an appropriate match of technology and leadership style is obtained; at the boundary-spanning level, where an appropriate fit between the leadership style and the adoption of technological change is determined; and at the organizational leadership level, where strategic decision making is affected by technological constraints. All of these applications illustrate the uncertain and dynamic nature of technology and demonstrate how nursing leaders can be empowered to achieve goals more effectively by understanding existing technology. This use of technology by the leader is transformational in that employees are raised to "higher levels of motivation and morality" (Burns, 1978, p. 20) by feeling that the leadership style is tailored to the type of work that is being done in their unit.

Unit-Level Match of Technology and Leadership Style

The appropriate match of technology and leadership style at the unit level will be presented in three situations: the nursing unit, the traditional professional bureaucracy, and the newly evolving nursing entrepreneurial organization. These situations illustrate the variety of technologies of which the transformational leader must be aware in selecting the appropriate leadership style to empower nursing in promotion of optimal performance and outcomes.

Nursing unit perspective

As discussed previously, research on technology of nursing units has indicated that the proper fit of technology and structure improves operating efficiency. Structure is defined as the allocation of work roles and administrative mechanisms to control work activities. Many of the structural aspects of nursing units, such as policies and involvement in decision making, are determined by the nurse leader. Thus the leadership style of the nurse leader should be consistent with the technology on the unit.

Several models* have been developed that suggest technological instability and variability can be matched with appropriate levels of subordinate participation in job-related tasks and decision making to improve the unit's operation and patient care outcomes. The Alexander and colleagues' model suggests that on nursing units with high instability, as characterized by more emergency situations and more requirements for frequent nursing observations and technical monitoring, leaders should use a more task-oriented style that requires more consultation and supervision of tasks. Conversely, if technological instability is low, leaders should use a more participative style, allowing subordinates to make independent decisions and being less consultative concerning job-related tasks.

Similarly, on nursing units with high technological variability, where tasks and patient diagnoses vary widely, personnel should be involved in defining tasks and determining how the work unit is organized. On the other hand, where variability among patients is low, leaders should decide on the way the tasks are accomplished without input from the staff. An additional responsibility of the transformational leader is to ensure that the unit members have enough information to understand the decisions being made. For nursing, this decision making is related to the delivery of patient care on the unit (Galbraith, 1972).

---

* Alexander and Bauerschmidt, 1987; Alexander and Randolph, 1985; Comstock and Scott, 1977; Kovner, 1966; Loveridge, 1988; Mark, 1983; Schoonhoven, 1981

On an intensive care unit where instability is high, the staff would not be involved with the definition of tasks that need to be accomplished, but due to high technological variability they would be involved with decision making concerning the organization of the tasks already defined by the nurse leader. On the other hand, in a newborn nursery where instability and variability in patients is low, the leadership style and attitude toward participation should be such that nursing personnel would not need to work closely with one another but would have input into overall decision making and task definition.

Professional bureaucracy perspective

Most health care organizations are professional bureaucracies. These organizations are complex and have fewer rules and more decentralization than other bureaucratic organizations (Mintzberg, 1979). The professional organizational members are concerned with the profession, and as a result they often overlook organizational strategic problems and opportunities. To empower nursing in this situation, the transformational leader is challenged to direct and coordinate these professionals, while enabling them to maintain their desired level of professional autonomy.

Nursing as a professional group is the largest component of the health care organization. Nursing carries out much of the work of the organization and has extensive autonomy to perfect skills, free from administrative interference. The leader in this situation must often adopt a *laissez-faire* style. At the same time, a *laissez-faire* leader must establish a coordination system that can handle incompetent or unconscientious professionals, allocate scarce resources, and promote innovation among professionals. Achieving this balance is not an easy task for the leader, but it is essential if the nursing organization is to accomplish goals for quality of care in a cost effective manner. This imperative of meeting professional desires for autonomy within traditional bureaucratic organizations is even more important as TQM (total quality management) and restructured organizational designs are implemented in health care settings (Arikian, 1991; Strasen, 1991).

The case of an administrator of an ambulatory surgery service within a traditional medical center illustrates this process. In this situation the administrator is dealing with the numerous professionals and their associated technologies necessary to provide a variety of outpatient surgical procedures: tonsillectomies, D&Cs, cataract removals, and minor orthopedic procedures, to name a few. This administrative leader must provide the medical and paraprofessional employees with adequate equipment and support services to provide patient care and give them latitude to make clinical decisions to ensure the quality of the care. At the same time, the leader must establish monitoring mechanisms for the quality assurance and performance appraisal systems; must acquire the financial and human resources needed to support the desired level of clinical practice; and must provide informational linkages so that the ambulatory surgery service works in harmony with the traditional surgical services.

Entrepreneurial perspective

In the current health care environment, more and more nurses are turning to entrepreneurial endeavors. These endeavors are distinguished from traditional bureaucratic health care organizations by different technologies. The technologies within entrepreneurial firms are such that the leader assumes risks and carries out the activities of the business using new, innovative methods. Examples of nurse entrepreneurial efforts include homeless clinics, primary care clinics, and provision of tertiary care in the home.

For these institutions the transformational leader can obtain direction for empowerment from emerging organizational literature. Covin and Slevin (1988) studied the top management's orientation in 80 U.S. business firms. From the collected data, the firms were designated as either entrepreneurial or bureaucratic. The results indicated two types of top performing firms: entrepreneurial top-management styles with flexible, organic firms, or conservative bureaucratic firms with inflexible, mechanistic top-management styles.

The implication for nursing leaders in entrepreneurial units is that the leadership style must match the technology of the work to be accomplished. The entrepreneurial style works well if the organization is innovative and open to a high degree of participation, a low specification of tasks, and few procedures. The conservative style, on the other hand, is appropriate in the bureaucratic, mechanistic settings that have little participation, high task specification, and many procedures.

Boundary-Spanning Level of Match Between Adoption of Technological Change and Leadership Style

Boundary spanners are employees who operate at the edge of the organization, performing tasks that relate to external organizational elements (Leifer and Delbecq, 1978). The more dynamic and complex the environment, the greater the importance of the boundary-spanning role. New ideas are introduced by individuals within the nursing organization who serve the role of bringing in environmental information as well as by new nurses in the organization. New ideas also are generated through research, serendipity, and practice. Boundary spanning involves scanning the environment for threats and opportunities as well as buffering or protecting the organization from environmental influences.

Whether the nursing leader is the boundary spanner or designates others to perform this task, the leader is responsible for obtaining and using the information from scanning activities to formulate policy for the organization. Additionally, the leader uses the buffering activities to control the impact that environmental changes could have on the institution and to allow the organization to operate somewhat as a closed system.

The leadership style determines how the scanning and buffering activities within the organization respond to the technological change. Burns and Stalker (1961) found that organizations operating in stable environments performed better with high levels of rules and procedures (formalization) and with centralized decision making (a great deal of buffering). In rapidly changing environments, a more flexible and adaptable style was needed. Nursing operates within a rapidly changing environment and thus performs better when professionals within the organization are able to react and adapt quickly to environmentally induced technological change. This type of minimal supervision and maximum autonomy, in which professional nurses react to situations on their own, can cause conflict, fragmentation of services, and duplication of effort within the organization as a whole.

Lawrence and Lorsch (1967) described the mechanisms of differentiation and integration which can assist the leader in overcoming the shortfalls of adapting to technological change to achieve the most efficient response. Differentiation through specialization of tasks allows the organization to respond quickly and appropriately to environmental changes. Integration through mechanisms of open and timely communication overcomes the problems of conflict and inefficiencies that may result from nurses "doing their own thing."

Additionally, whether the leader allows for rapid acquisition of new ideas, or if more buffering is used to slow the introduction of the ideas, the change is not simply absorbed (Hall, 1991). The leader must use political savvy to advocate or moderate the change. This aspect of leadership requires constant awareness of the changes in the technological environment of nursing and of the capabilities of the institution's resources. For example, the rapid computerization of nursing activities during the 1980s caused nursing leaders to adapt to maintain their goals of high quality care. The response was quite different in an urban medical center where advanced treatment modalities were used than in a small rural institution that provided mostly primary care. The leader in the urban organization was continually acquiring and adapting to new technologies. The leader in the rural organization was buffering the organization from these changes so that their introduction could be done with adequate control over limited human and fiscal resources.

Organizational Level Match of Strategic Leadership and Technology

Strategy formulation in health care organizations is the process by which top management develops the general program of action and designates that emphasis be placed upon and resources be used toward the attainment of overall organizational goals. The intent in this process is to give direction to those controlling human and material resources so that the objective of quality, cost-effective, and accessible health care is achieved. Though strategic direction is often established at the top management level, the impact is seen at the unit level.

The role of technology in the strategy formulation process may be twofold. A certain strategic choice may necessitate selection of a specific technology (Leatt and Fried, 1988). For example, in a large metropolitan area with a growing population of people with HIV related disease, a health care institution found that this population has multiple health problems with frequent admissions for extended periods of time. The leadership team decided that care of patients with HIV related disease was an important part of its mission but was concerned about the effect the cost of caring for these patients would have on the institution's overall performance. The leadership team reviewed the research and discovered that case management of these patients is cost effective. Thus the technology of case management was used to follow these patients from diagnosis through treatment and death.

On the other hand, a new, internally developed technology may cause the leadership team to alter their strategic direction (Leatt and Fried, 1988). For example, the obstetrical department within a hospital may develop a concept of care that reduces the time of hospitalization to less than 12 hours following delivery. This change in technology would necessitate the leadership team to make strategic decisions to market this service but also establish a community outreach service to support families who need additional care within the home.

An additional aspect of strategy formulation that is important for the transformational leader is the role of consensus builder. Consensus is the agreement of all parties to a group decision. The process of reaching consensus occurs after deliberation and discussion of the pros and cons of an issue. Consensus is important in the strategic selection of technology. Dess and Origer (1987) presented a review of the literature on consensus building and proposed several statements to explain how environmental dimensions, which include stability and certainty of technology, impact on the consensus building process. They proposed that the more dynamic and complex the environment is, the less consensus exists on organizational goals and competitive mechanisms. But they additionally proposed that firms that exist in the dynamic, unstable environments with limited resources perform better if there is a high level of *internal* working together (integration). Though these statements have not been fully tested, the implication for nursing leaders is that consensus is necessary for strategic goal formulation and achievement, even though it is difficult to reach in the current health care environment. Given this fact, the nursing leader must use a style that promotes a high degree of integration, coordination, and communication among the various nursing constituencies.

□ *Implications for Nursing*

Technology is an environmental factor that impacts upon the selection of appropriate leadership styles. The importance of technology can be discussed from both internal and external organizational views. Thus the transformational nursing leader must ensure that mechanisms are in place for constant monitoring of the internal and external technologies.

The idea of situational nursing leadership and the appropriate match between technology and nursing leadership styles are important. If the nursing leadership styles at the unit, boundary-spanning, and strategy formulation levels are congruent with the technology, better decisions will be made and the effectiveness of nursing organizations will improve.

□ *Application to Nursing: Case Study*

Veronica Jones recently became the head nurse on an 18-bed child psychiatric unit in a 250-bed psychiatric facility. Prior to taking the job she had worked part-time on the unit but was asked to assume the position after the previous head nurse decided to resign following a maternity leave. The children on the unit are both male and female and range in age from 6 to 12 years. A variety of psychiatric diagnoses are treated, including behavior disorders, schizophrenia, and autism. The average census is 12.

Veronica is interested in achieving high quality of care within the constraints of a tight budget. The staff on the unit consists of five full time RNs, four part-time RNs, four LPNs, and 10 mental health specialists. An external agency is available for staffing, but the hospital administration has discouraged its use. The nursing staff on the unit operates in a functional manner; the RNs coordinate the team, the LPNs administer medications, and the mental health specialists assist with the children's activities of daily living and provide for the supervision of their behavior.

Veronica's assessment of the technology on the unit is a relatively low degree of instability and variability but a high level of uncertainty among the children. For example, 10-year-old Phillip was admitted to the unit because of his inability to make satisfactory behavioral adjustments to school and home. His teacher reported that he was always aggressive toward other children and that his behavior was often bizarre. His mother reported that she was unable to control him at home and that he was very restless, blinked his eyes often, and masturbated frequently. Three days after admission, Phillip's inappropriate behavior continued on the unit; he kicked over the trash can and began shouting while the other children watched television.

The nature of Phillip's psychiatric problem was complex and difficult to understand, and it ultimately was attributed to his relationship with a chronically depressed mother and hostile, aggressive father.

With this type of patient and the resulting level of technological uncertainty in planning for his care, Veronica believed that a high degree of structure (formalization) was required for the nursing staff to deliver quality care. To implement this level of formalization, Veronica insisted that the staff follow unit procedures for use of the composure room and completion of process modules by the children when disruptive behavior occurred. She also implemented a communication book and required the staff to read it daily.

Veronica realized that most of the children on this unit have similar diagnoses that are low in variability with predictable treatment plans (low instability). She knew that with this type of technological instability and variability, the best care is given with high levels of vertical participation coupled with low levels of horizontal participation. Through weekly meetings Veronica promoted a great deal of interchange among the medical staff, nursing management, and nursing staff on decisions related to changing overall treatment programs (such as implementing a behavior modification program). She also established a group of nurses to prepare time schedules and to make suggestions for changing the assignment patterns.

Additionally, Veronica met with the medical staff to set up a situation in which the nursing and medical staffs could act independently of administration in implementing the treatment plans for the children. She was thus able to assure the nursing staff of minimal supervision of their independent judgments.

A JCAHO visit is scheduled for the hospital 6 months after Veronica becomes head nurse. She is concerned about the nursing documentation of plans of care on the unit.

Questions for Discussion

1. What sort of leadership should Veronica provide to address her concerns about the upcoming JCAHO visit?
2. Given the technology on this children's psychiatric unit, would Veronica's style of leadership need to change if the mix of nursing personnel change? If there were more RNS? If there were more paraprofessionals?
3. How would the technology on this unit change if the unit was also a forensic unit and admitted childhood delinquents for evaluation?
4. What alternative nursing assignment patterns might be appropriate for this unit?

5. What effect would the addition of a clinical nurse specialist have on the technology-leadership match on this unit?
6. How would this unit change if the strategic direction of the hospital changed to one of increased community based services?

References

Alexander, J.W. and Bauerschmidt, A.D. (1987). Implications for nursing administration of the relationship of technology and structure to quality of care. *Nursing Administration Quarterly, 11*(4), 1-10.

Alexander, J.W. and Mark, B. (1990). Technology and structure of nursing organizations. *Nursing and Health Care, 11*(4), 195-199.

Alexander, J.W. and Randolph, W.A. (1985). The fit between technology and structure as a predictor of performance in nursing subunits. *Academy of Management Journal, 28,* 844-859.

Arikian, V.L. (1991). Total quality management: applications to nursing service. *Journal of Nursing Administration, 21*(6), 46-50.

Burns, J.M. (1978). *Leadership*. New York: Harper & Row.

Burns, T. and Stalker, G. M. (1961). *The management of innovation*. London: Tavistock Publications.

Child, J. (1972). Organizational structure, environment, and performance: The role of strategic choice. *Sociology, 6*(1), 1-22.

Comstock, D.E., and Scott, W.R. (1977). Technology and the structure of subunits: distinguishing individual and work group differences. *Administrative Science Quarterly, 22,* 177-202.

Covin, J.G. and Slevin, D.P. (1988). The influence of organizational structure on the utility of an entrepreneurial top management style. *Journal of Management Studies, 25,* 217-234.

Dess, G.G. and Origer, N.K. (1987). Environment, structure, and consensus in strategy formulation: a conceptual integration. *Academy of Management Review, 12,* 313-330.

Etzioni, A. (1965). Dual leadership in complex organizations. *American Sociological Review, 30,* 688-698.

Fiedler, F.E. (1967). *A theory of leadership effectiveness*. New York: McGraw-Hill.

Fiedler, F.E. (1972). The effects of leadership training and experience: a contingency model explanation. *Administrative Science Quarterly, 17,* 453-470.

Fry, L.W., and Slocum, J.W. (1984). Technology, structure and workgroup effectiveness: a test of a contingency model. *Academy of Management Journal, 27,* 221-246.

Galbraith, J. (1972). Organization design: an information processing view. In Lorsch, J. and Lawrence, P., editors: *Organization planning: cases and concepts.* Homewood, Ill.: Irwin-Dorsey.

Hall, R.H. (1991). *Organizations: structures, processes, and outcomes* (ed. 5). Englewood Cliffs, N.J.: Prentice Hall.

Hasenfeld, Y. (1983). *Human service organizations.* Englewood Cliffs, N.J.: Prentice-Hall.

Ito, J.K. and Peterson, R. (1986). Effects of task difficulty and interunit interdependence on information processing systems. *Academy of Management Journal, 29,* 139-149.

Kovner, A. (1966). *The nursing unit: a technological perspective.* Unpublished doctoral dissertation, University of Pittsburgh.

Lawrence, P.R. and Lorsch, J.W. (1967). *Organization and environment: managing differentiation and integration.* Boston: Division of Research, Harvard Business School.

Leatt, P. and Fried, B. (1988). Technology and human resource management. In *Strategic management of human resources in health services organizations.* Fottler, M.D., Hernandez, S.R., and Joiner, C.L., editors: New York: John Wiley & Sons.

Leavitt, J.H. (1965). Applied organizational change in industry: Structural, technological, and humanistic approaches. In *Handbook of organizations.* March, J.G., editor: Chicago: Rand McNally College Publishing.

Leifer, R. and Delbecq, A. (1978). Organizational/environmental interchange: a model of boundary spanning activity. *Academy of Management Review, 3,* 40-49.

Loveridge, C.E. (1988). Contingency theory: explaining staff nurse retention. *Journal of Nursing Administration, 18*(6), 22-25.

Mark, B. (1983). Task and structural correlates of organizational effectiveness in private psychiatric hospitals. *Health Services Research, 20,* 199-224.

Mark, B. (1989). Structural contingency theory. In Henry, B., Arndt, C., DiVincenti, M., and Marriner-Tomey, A., editors: *Dimensions of nursing administration.* Boston: Blackwell Scientific Publications.

Mintzberg, H. (1979). *The structuring of organizations.* Englewood Cliffs, N.J.: Prentice Hall.

Overton, P., Schneck, R., and Hazlett, C. (1977). An empirical study of the technology of nursing subunits. *Administrative Science Quarterly, 22,* 203-219.

Perrow, C. (1965). Hospitals, technology, structure, and goals. In *Handbook of organizations.* March, J.G., editor: Chicago: Rand McNally College Publishing.

Perrow, C. (1967). A framework for comparative analysis of organizations. *American Sociology Review, 32,* 194-208.

Peters, P. and Austin, N. (1985). *A passion for excellence.* New York: Random House.

Schoonhoven, C.B. (1981). Problems with contingency theory: testing assumptions hidden within the language of contingency theory. *Administative Science Quartely, 26,* 349 – 377.

Strasen, L. (1991). Redesigning hospital around patients and technology. *Nursing Economics, 9,* 233-238.

Verran, J.A. and Reid, P.J. (1987). Replicated testing of the nursing technology model. *Nursing Research, 36,* 190-194.

Woodward, J. (1965). *Industrial organizations: theory and practice.* New York: McGraw-Hill.

Yukl, G.A. (1981). *Leadership in organization.* Englewood Cliffs, N.J.: Prentice Hall.

11

VIRGINIA RICHARDSON

Decision Making

CHAPTER OBJECTIVES

☐ Discuss components of leader behavior.

☐ Describe type theory.

☐ Identify four major decision-making models and summarize their important points.

☐ Identify four leadership styles.

☐ Describe the four basic decision-making patterns that result in basic leadership styles.

B ehavior is a reflection of the decisions that people make. An understanding of the decision-making process is necessary for understanding the behaviors of individuals and of complex organizations. March and Simon (1958) made the first attempt to explain the behavior of organizations in terms of their decision-making processes. Cyert and March (1963) expanded upon their work.

Gardner (1986) identified two tasks of leadership to be goal setting and motivating. Goal setting can be done in a variety of ways. One leader may choose to impose his or her vision of what the group or organization can be at its best, while another may help to solve problems. The task of motivating is accomplished by aligning individual and group goals. A leader is able to determine what motivates individuals and then channel these things for the good of the organization. The followers can then make significant contributions to the organization.

Stogdill (1948) identified two components of leader behavior. One type of leader behavior is concerned with task activities, such as setting goals, giving directions, and organizing the work setting. The other type of leader behavior has to do with interpersonal activities, such as cooperating with co-workers, guiding the work group's interactions and providing psychological support to individual group members or to the group as a whole. Blake and Mouton (1962) found that an effective leader exhibits both types of behavior.

Stogdill (1948) found in his research studies that there were no universal characteristics of leaders to differentiate them from followers. These research findings did not support the previously held beliefs that there were special characteristics or traits that made leaders successful. As a result, situational and contingency theories of leadership became popular.

Type Theory

Freund (1988) has assessed decision-making styles using Jung's theory of psychological types, the interpretation of Jung's theory by Myers and Briggs, and the development of the Myers-Briggs Type Indicator (MBTI). The MBTI measures the way people take in information and form conclusions about the information (Myers and McCaulley, 1985).

The MBTI has been categorized as a psychological test, but it is not diagnostic or evaluative. It has been used in industry for a long time and is now being used more extensively in the health care field. The MBTI is a tool that can help individuals understand their own strengths and limitations as well as how they differ from others. There are no right or wrong answers, but only differences in perception and judgment. In work situations the MBTI has been used to help individuals work with and understand other people.

Type theory refers to Jung's theory of psychological type. Jung observed that people prefer to perceive and make judgments according to patterns. These patterns are referred to as psychological types. The perception patterns are sensing or intuition, and the two judgment patterns are thinking and feeling. Everyone uses all four processes, but individuals differ in their preferences and skills in using the processes.

Myers and Briggs identified four dimensions of psychological type: a perception function, a judgment function, an attitude toward life, and an orientation to the outer world (Myers and McCaulley, 1985). These four dimensions each contain polar opposites: two opposite perception processes, sensing and intuition; two opposite judgment processes, thinking and feeling; two opposite attitudes toward life, extroversion and introversion; and two opposite orientations to the outer world, perceiving and judging (Myers and McCaulley, 1985).

In decision-making situations it is important for leaders to understand their type preferences so they can realize the limitations of their information processing and the fact that they will come to conclusions based on certain standards. If leaders are aware of these personal limitations they can consult with people of the opposite type to broaden their scope and bring into consideration the other type of information.

Another way of viewing leaders and followers is in terms of brain hemisphere predominance. Much has been written recently about the split brain theory (Adams, 1986; Gazzaniga, 1975; Sperry, 1975). The brain consists of right and left hemispheres, which are responsible for different functions. The right brain is used for intuition, insight, visualization, and spatial perception. The left brain is used for speaking, writing, reading, analyzing, judging, and mathematical ability. Both sides of the brain are used, but in most individuals one side is preferred over the other. Using both sides of the brain is referred to as "whole brain thinking," and this allows for more options and resources (Adams, 1986).

Decision-Making Models

Leaders spend much of their time making decisions, whether routine or of major importance. No single decision-making model is appropriate for every decision-making venture. There are many different types of models, and a leader should employ several of them.

Much of the work of behavioral scientists has consisted of developing normative models describing how people should make decisions. Janis and Mann (1977) identified what people of all ages do when making personal, organizational, or political decisions of serious consequence. Serious decisions were described as those made by leaders of organizations or members of executive committees. Serious personal decisions govern such questions as marriage, changing jobs, and buying a home. Janis and Mann's (1977) study did not apply to minor, everyday decisions.

One of the major concepts of the Janis and Mann (1977) decision-making model is psychological stress. Contemplating a major decision inevitably produces stress in an individual. Signs of stress include apprehension and a desire to escape from having to make the choice. Epstein and Fenz (1965) investigated these stress symptoms in sky divers who had made over 100 jumps. The researchers determined by rating avoidance feelings that the time of greatest stress is when the parachutists make the original decision to jump, not when they are in the airplane before the jump. The feelings of avoidance decreased while on the flight. These feelings continued to decrease during the free fall, when the danger was the greatest.

Stress is also high when a person has to choose between two alternatives, both of which have some unpleasant consequences. Mann, Janis, and Chaplin (1969) studied coeds at the University of Melbourne in an experiment in which the coeds had to choose between two unpleasant forms of stimulation. Each subject's heart rate was monitored near the beginning of the session, during the predecision period, at the time the decision was made, and at the end of the session. The subjects' heart rates peaked during the time in which they had to announce their decision and then dropped off rapidly. Decisional conflict within an individual was described as simultaneously opposing tendencies to accept or reject a given course of action. Whenever making the decision was the focus of attention, symptoms experienced by the decision maker included hesitation, vacillation, feelings of uncertainty, and signs of emotional stress.

The Janis and Mann (1977) model attempted to specify the contrasting conditions that determined whether stress from decisional conflict would facilitate or interfere with information processing. A decision maker experiencing little conflict showed a low stress level and was unmotivated to give the decision much thought.

Five patterns of coping behavior that affect decision making were identified:
1. Vigilance (watchfulness) results in thorough information processing.
2. Unconflicted adherence occurred when the decision maker decided to continue what was being done and ignored all information about the risks or losses.
3. Unconflicted change occurred when the decision maker accepted the course of action that was most strongly recommended.

4. Defensive avoidance occurred when the decision maker evaded the conflict by procrastinating, shifting responsibility to someone else, or not heeding correct information.
5. Hypervigilance occurred when the decision maker searched for a way out of the dilemma, made a decision that provided immediate relief, but did not consider the consequences of the decision.

The first coping pattern is considered the best and will lead to making quality decisions. The other four coping patterns are defective, yet they are in the repertoire of every decision maker.

Another important concept of the model is commitment. Commitment was shown when the decision maker made a contract or took on an obligation to carry out a chosen course of action.

Janis and Mann (1977) developed a decisional balance sheet grid that indexed how thoroughly and accurately the decision maker explored all available positive and negative alternatives. The four main categories of the decisional balance sheet are the following:

1. *Utilitarian gains and losses for self.* This category includes all the expected effects of the decision with respect to personal objectives.
2. *Utilitarian gains and losses for significant others.* This category pertains to the goals of the decision maker and the group or organization represented by the decision maker.
3. *Self-approval or self-disapproval.* Self-image or self-esteem are factors in every decision.
4. *Approval or disapproval by significant others.* Another important consideration when making a decision is how that decision will be evaluated by those of importance to the decision maker.

Hoyt and Janis (1975) used the decisional balance sheet with 40 women who had signed up for an early morning exercise class. Twenty of the women were randomly chosen for a group that would use this balance sheet. They were asked to supply in the four categories all their positive and negative thoughts about being in the exercise class. The remaining 20 women were assigned to a different group and were asked to use the same four categories to record all the positive and negative aspects that would result from stopping smoking. The weekly attendance of those in the first group was much higher than of those in the second group. The conclusion was that when people make a decision by considering all the positive and negative aspects using the decisional balance sheet, they are more likely to be committed to the decision.

Hage (1980) examined decision making in the context of power processes. Leaders infrequently make high-risk decisions with long-term effects that could bring about changes in the coalition of power. Low-risk decisions are those that are routine, predictable, and likely to maintain the status quo of the organization. With high-risk decisions, not only are the outcomes uncertain, but the costs can be high, and experience with these decisions is limited because they are made infrequently. The example used by Hage (1980) to illustrate high risk involved IBM's decision to build the 360 computer. The necessary capital investment was very large, and if the product was not successful IBM would go bankrupt. The outcome of this decision affected almost every IBM employee. The decision was high-risk because there was a lack of data to support the idea that customers would accept the stiff start-up costs and change to this new series of computers. Once the decision had been made there could be no turning back.

Hage (1980) described the decision-making process for decisions of both high and low risk in terms of a trajectory or movement through the organization. Low-risk decisions occur rapidly, are announced on routing slips or memos, and are termed hierarchical trajectories because they are directed downward in the organization. High-risk decisions generate more discussions about handling the worries connected with the risk. High-risk decisions take longer because those involved need more time to make up their minds. This type of decision is described as having a network trajectory because the idea moves back and forth among individuals or groups within the organization. The more issues that must be considered in making the final decision, the more complex are the trajectories.

One of the latest contingency theories to be introduced is the Vroom and Yetton (1973) decision process theory. Contingency theories view the consequences of leader actions as contingent on situational or organizational conditions.

The Vroom-Yetton (1973) normative model outlines ways of characterizing problem situations and then determines appropriate decision-making styles. The leader first answers seven yes-no questions that measure the situation's attributes. Four of the seven questions pertain to the acceptance of the solution by subordinates. The other three questions pertain to the quality of the decision. The questions are these:
- How important is the quality of the decision?
- Does the leader have enough information to make a good decision?
- Is the problem structured?
- Is acceptance of the decision by the followers critical to its implementation?
- If the leader makes an autocratic decision, is it reasonably certain that the followers would accept the decision?
- Do followers share the organizational goals to be reached by solving this problem?
- Is conflict among followers likely to occur in preferred solutions?

Various combinations of answers to these yes-no questions represent different sets of leadership decision styles. Five such leadership decision styles range from autocratic to consultative to group. An autocratic decision style (AI and AII) includes minimal involvement of the followers in the decision-making process and is usually the fastest process. The consultative decision style (CI and CII) has some degree of follower involvement. Group decision style (GII) involves followers the most and is usually the slowest process.

The Vroom and Yetton (1973) decision-making model is usually depicted as a decision tree. By progressively moving along the branches as the seven questions are answered, one reaches the final node or intersection that identifies the decision making style.

Vroom and Yetton (1973) developed a set of seven rules for choosing among the decision-making styles.

1. **Information Rule.** If the leader does not have enough information or expertise to solve the problem alone or if the quality of the decision is important, then AI is eliminated as a possible decision-making style.

2. **Goal Congruence Rule.** If the quality of the decision is important and if the followers do not share the organization's goal of solving this problem, then GII is eliminated from the possible decision styles.

3. **Unstructured Problem Rule.** If the leader does not know what information is needed or where the information can be located, then interaction with the followers who have that information will be the best method to produce a high level solution. AI, AII, and CI are eliminated as possible decision styles.

4. **Acceptance Rule.** If follower acceptance of the decision is critical for effective implementation and if the leader does not know whether an autocratic decision would be accepted, then AI and AII are eliminated as possible decision styles.

5. **Conflict Rule.** If an autocratic decision might not be accepted (although the followers might disagree about the solution) and follower acceptance of the decision is critical, then possible decision styles AI, AII, and CI are eliminated.

6. **Fairness Rule.** If acceptance of the decision is critical but the quality is unimportant, then AI, AII, CI, and CII are eliminated.

7. **Acceptance Priority Rule.** If acceptance of the decision is critical and subordinates can be relied upon, AI, AII, CI, and CII are eliminated as decision choices.

After all seven rules have been applied to a problem, a list of possible decision styles is formulated. When more than one decision style is available to solve a problem, the solution requiring the least amount of time is generally chosen.

Fourteen terminal nodes are generated when using this model. Each of the 14 nodes represents a particular type of problem and includes decision styles acceptable for solving the problem. This model can also be written into a computer program, and the questions then become prompts in the program.

The model identifies the level of participation of subordinates involved in making the decision but does not prescribe the social interactions among the decision makers (Tjosvold, Wedley, and Field, 1986). The Vroom-Yetton (1973) decision-making model was used with 58 managers enrolled in an executive MBA program to see whether constructive controversy (skilled discussion of opposing positions) can supplement the model. Tjosvold, Wedley, and Field (1986) found that both the Vroom-Yetton model and constructive controversy are significantly related to successful decision making.

Heller (1973) developed a sociotechnical contingency model for analyzing decision-making style using five clearly defined alternatives. These five methods form what is called an Influence-Power Continuum (IPC). The IPC is used to analyze how decisions are made in terms of the distribution of power, but not what decisions are made. The IPC is shown in the box on p. 161.

These five IPC alternatives cover a wide range of behavior, even including delegation as a means of making a decision. This is an extension of previously discussed leadership styles in decision making, which have ranged from autocratic to democratic.

Heller (1973) determined that managers use leadership styles that are contingent upon their awareness of different situations. When the decision is not particularly important for either the organization or the individual leader, both autocratic and delegation leadership styles seem to be used. This suggests that leaders think relatively unimportant decisions can be made using decision methods requiring little time.

Hersey and Blanchard (1988) developed the Situational Leadership Model, which determined that there are different patterns of leader behavior. According to this model, there is no single best way to influence people. The leadership style is determined according to the readiness level of the followers, as illustrated in Figure 11-1.

Situational Leadership is based on an interplay among (1) the amount of guidance and direction (task behavior) a leader gives, (2) the amount of socioemotional support (relationship behavior) a leader provides, and (3) the readiness level that followers exhibit in performing a specific task, function, or objective (Hersey and Blanchard, 1988).

Task behavior is defined as the extent to which the leader identifies the duties and responsibilities of an individual or group (Hersey and Blanchard, 1988).

Relationship behavior is defined as the extent to which the leader engages in bilateral or multilateral communication. Examples of this include active listening, giving support, and providing feedback (Hersey and Blanchard, 1988).

Style 1 of leader behavior, as depicted in Figure 11-1, is referred to as "telling." Telling is providing specific instructions and closely supervising performance.

Style 2 is "selling"; the leader explains decisions and provides opportunities for clarification.

Methods of Making Decisions (The Influence-Power Continuum)

The five methods are defined for each manager as follows:

"In this form we are concerned with the management skill called 'decision-making'. This term includes the process leading up to the final decision, and advice or recommendations which are usually accepted also count as decisions for the purposes of this research. Many alternative methods of decision-making exist, among them are those described below. All have been shown to be widely used and effective."

1. *Own decision without* detailed explanation.

   Decisions are made by managers without previous discussion or consultation with subordinates. No special meeting or memorandum is used to explain the decision.

2. *Own decision with* detailed explanation.

   Same as above, but afterwards managers explain the problem and the reasons for their choice in a memo or in a special meeting.

3. *Prior consultation* with subordinate.

   Before the decision is made, the manager explains the problem to his subordinate and asks his advice and help. The manager then makes the decision by himself. His final choice may, or may not, reflect his subordinate's influence.

4. *Joint decision-making* with subordinate.

   Managers and their subordinates together analyze the problem and come to a decision. The subordinates usually have as much influence over the final choice as the managers. Where there are more than two individuals in the discussion, the decision of the majority is accepted more often than not.

5. *Delegation* of decision to subordinate.

   A manager asks his subordinate to make the decision regarding a particular problem. He may or may not request the subordinate to report the decision to him. The manager seldom vetoes the subordinate's decisions.

From Heller, F. (1973). Leadership, decision making, and contingency theory, *Industrial Relations,* 12(2), p. 188. Used with permission.

Style 3 is "participating"; the leader shares ideas and facilitates decision making.

Style 4 is "delegating"; the leader turns over the responsibility for decisions and their implementation to subordinates.

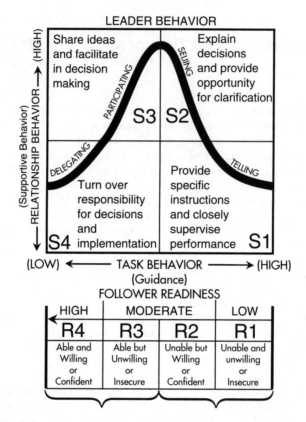

Fig. 11-1. Situational leadership. From Hersey, P. & Blanchard, K.: *Management of organizational behavior,* ed 5, New Jersey, 1988, Prentice Hall. Used by permission of Leadership Studies, Inc.

Another component of this model is follower readiness. Hersey and Blanchard (1988) define readiness as the extent to which a follower has the ability and willingness to accomplish a specific task. Followers' levels of readiness vary, depending on the tasks they are asked to perform.

Follower readiness is divided into four levels:

1. **Readiness level one.** The follower lacks ability, commitment, motivation, and confidence to follow the leader.
2. **Readiness level two.** The follower lacks ability but is motivated and confident as long as the leader continues to provide guidance.
3. **Readiness level three.** The follower has the ability to perform the task but is unwilling to do so and is insecure in doing it alone.

4. **Readiness level four.** The follower has the ability to perform, is committed, and is confident about doing it.

The leader provides direction to the followers at the lower levels of readiness. At the higher levels of readiness the followers become much more responsible for their own task direction.

The curved line through the four leadership styles shown in Figure 11-1 represents the combination of task behavior and relationship behavior, which is a combination of high probability (Hersey and Blanchard, 1988). To determine the amount of task behavior and relationship behavior for a situation, one can identify a point on the readiness continuum, which represents follower readiness to perform a task, and draw a perpendicular line from that point to intersect with the curved line that indicates leader behavior (Hersey and Blanchard, 1988). This point identifies the most appropriate amount of task behavior, relationship behavior, and leader behavior for a given situation.

Take as an example the case of a leader evaluating a secretary's phone skills. Having recognized which aspect of the secretary's job is to be influenced, the leader gauges the ability and motivation (readiness level) of the secretary. Next, the leader determines which leader behavior is appropriate for influencing each of these areas. It is determined that the secretary's readiness level in terms of answering phones is low; i.e., the secretary is unwilling or unable to follow through in this area. Using the four leadership styles presented in Figure 11-1 the leader would know to use a directive telling (S1) when working with this secretary. More time would have to be spent training the employee. As the secretary demonstrates the ability to answer the phone in the desired manner, the leader will move on to the leadership behavior associated with selling.

Deitzer and Krigline (1988) discussed how the tensions of decision making can be relieved and the quality of decisions can be improved. One of their recommendations is to become very familiar with the pros and cons of the issue and then delay making the decision until the next day ("sleeping on it"). After a night's sleep people are more physically relaxed, more anxiety-free, and better able to be objective.

Deitzer and Krigline (1988) categorize problems as follows: those that have already occurred, including crises; those that can be anticipated but not prevented; and those that can be prevented if a decision is made early enough.

The decision-making process involves gathering all the data about the problem, writing down all the possible solutions, eliminating those that will not work, and then acting on the decision.

Steiner (1965) discussed how organizational environments can encourage creativity among leaders and followers. Organizations that were considered creative had the following characteristics: (1) open channels of communication were maintained; (2) management was tolerant of risk-taking; (3) ideas were evaluated on their own merits, independent of the originator; and (4) participative decision making was encouraged.

The creative process has been described by Shapero (1985) as having four steps: (1) preparation, (2) incubation, (3) illumination, and (4) verification. Preparation begins when a problem is perceived and is not solved by direct action. The problem is explored from different angles, which may include discussions with other workers, library research, and free thinking. The incubation process is subconscious and actually appears to work best when the decision maker is focused on something else. The sudden insight into the solution is called illumination. The final step, verification, is when the creative idea must pass the tests of reality, utility, and acceptance.

Glassman (1989) discussed the use of brainstorming to generate new ideas to help with problem solving. To brainstorm, employees were divided into groups of five to seven people, and they would generate a variety of ideas. The ideas were not evaluated until they all had been listed.

Brainwriting is related to brainstorming. People in groups write out their own ideas. Because the ideas remain anonymous, Glassman (1988) found that more ideas were generated than with brainstorming. Brainstorming and brainwriting were used as part of a four-step process in problem solving. After 20 to 30 minutes had been spent in brainstorming and brainwriting, the group would spend 20 minutes generating crazy ideas. A game was then played, the object of which was to make the ideas from the other team appear as useful as possible for solving the problem. The last step in the process was called idea-gallery brainwriting, and there were two ways of doing this. First the leader would write down six to eight problem statements on individual flip charts. The participants would walk around the room, and each would write ideas and solutions on the flip charts. Next, the participants would sit for 30 to 40 minutes and write ideas on individual index cards. The members then exchanged cards, writing down new ideas as they occurred to them. The index cards were then placed around the room so the participants could see them as they would form their problem-solving proposals.

The Claus-Bailey (1975) Model for Decision Making was developed to assist students in systematizing the decision-making process. This model is a cybernetic system that uses feedback or evaluation of the decision to enable the decision maker to alter the results of the decision as needed. The Claus-Bailey (1975) model includes the following 10 steps, which are usually depicted in a linear fashion.

1. Define the overall needs, goals, and purposes of the system or of the individuals within that system. (Ideally this would have been done before the problem developed.)

2. Define the problem. This is critical in ensuring that decision makers focus on the correct problem.
3. Having identified the problem, examine the constraints, capabilities, and resources available to aid in solving the problem.
4. Determine what approach or framework will be used to solve the problem. If the problem is complex, people may need to solve many sub-problems or make numerous decisions before the larger, overall problem can be solved.
5. State the expected outcomes or desired accomplishments resulting from the decision.
6. Use past experiences, obtain the opinions of experts, or use group process techniques such as brainstorming to list alternative solutions that could be achieved.
7. Analyze all the options that have been generated against the objectives and expected outcomes identified in step 5.
8. Determine the best problem-solving option, which is usually the alternative that most closely matches the objectives. Rules are applied in this step if there is a tie between alternatives or if the decision maker did not think this was the best solution. Decision rules are based on the overall purposes identified in step 1. Does the alternative match or fit with the overall purpose? If not, a different alternative should be selected. The policies of the institution are commonly used for decision rules.
9. Implement the decision. This involves careful planning of objectives, policies and procedures, and strategies that will be necessary for the decision to be realized. Included in planning should be a warning system to alert the decision maker if the implementation is headed for difficulties.
10. Analyze the effectiveness of the selected course of action. The performance results are evaluated against standards developed earlier. Positive feedback indicates that the selected alternative was appropriate and the problem is solved; negative feedback indicates that the chosen alternative did not solve the problem. If necessary, the decision could be put through the decision-making sequence again, starting at the point where difficulties arose.

Problem solving can involve anywhere from three steps to a large number of steps to reach a solution. Several authors (Scharf, 1985; Blai, 1986; and Segall and Meyers, 1988) propose very similar methods for solving problems. Each one identifies a different number of steps in the process, with varying degrees of specificity within each step. All three concur in identifying the problem, naming it, determining how to solve it by thinking of many solutions, implementing a solution, and having a contingency solution available if needed.

Leadership Styles

Rodrigues (1988) proposed that organizations at different stages of development need leaders with different traits, abilities, and behaviors. Three organizational stages were identified as the problem-solving stage, the implementation stage, and the stable stage. The three respective types of leaders were the innovator, the implementor, and the pacifier.

The innovator was characterized by having a need for competition and success, and by always searching for new ideas. The implementor was characterized by the need to control and influence situations and to make decisions. The pacifier was characterized by the need for a friendly environment, having the ability to pacify important individuals, and choosing to decentralize decision making.

An organization that needs new ideas or is operating in a time of crisis would function more effectively by employing a leader with the characteristics of the innovator. This individual is forceful, creative, and able to sell new ideas.

After the ideas are sold to the organization, a leader with the characteristics of the implementor would better help the organization achieve its goals. The implementor is very organized and capable of getting the job done, bringing the organization to the stable stage.

At the stable stage the most effective leader would be the pacifier. Followers of such a leader usually feel comfortable doing any task required of them.

Rodrigues (1988) developed a questionnaire to help managers determine whether an individual's characteristics were those of an innovator, implementor, or pacifier. Both the individual in question and the institutional manager would use the 31 questions on this questionnaire to rate the prospective leader.

Some leaders will be dominant in one area, while some will be two-dimensional or three-dimensional. Mediocre ratings in a category might indicate that the individual will be an ineffective leader in that area, but a low score provides a sure indication that the individual will not be effective in that category.

Wiberg (1988) stated that there are four basic decision-making patterns, resulting in different leadership styles.

Leadership Style I — Founding. Leaders in this category have great skill at decision making by using theories, principles, and concepts, but they have a lot of difficulty with people problems.

Leadership Style II — Managing. These leaders are very thorough. They test all the possibilities and gather all the information, and their decisions are delayed until all the facts are known. These leaders are bureaucratic and organization-minded.

Leadership Style III — Developing. These leaders try to do what is right, they are team builders, and they are motivated by personal feelings. Style

III leaders adopt principles from traditional leadership models and hold fast to their models. They work well with people and have the ability to solve people problems with little effort.

Leadership Style IV — Inspiring. These leaders have difficulty following one of the other leadership models. They have highly personal guidance systems based on inspiration and intuition. They can solve problems rapidly, and they lead chiefly by example.

Leadership styles I and II may coexist in the same person. Their emphasis will be on objective, impersonal evaluation. This style of leadership can foster an exciting environment in which ideas can be discussed openly.

A blend of leadership styles II and III would produce a very realistic, practical leader with a down-to-earth approach to people and problems.

Leadership styles III and IV coexisting in one individual would yield an activist leader, achieving new things.

Leadership styles IV and I together would result in a very future-oriented leader. The future and preparation for it would be this leader's major concern. Such a leader would not be difficult to get along with because others' actions and thoughts are not of primary concern.

☐ *Implications for Nursing*

In discussing leadership traits, it becomes clear that there are no universal characteristics of leaders that differentiate them from followers. Determining psychological type is one way to help individuals understand their strengths and limitations in decision making. No single decision-making theory is appropriate for every situation, so knowledge of several theories will be helpful. Different types of leaders will be helpful in different types of situations. It is important for a nurse to know what type of leader he or she is, as well as the kinds of situations in which that type functions best.

☐ *Application to Nursing: Case Study*

The pediatric clinic in an 1100-bed hospital in a large midwestern city provides well and sick care to 8,000 children and adolescents. The nurse manager, who has been in her position for five years, reports to the newly hired clinical director. She is well-respected by her staff for her knowledge, skills, use of good judgment, good listening skills, caring attitude, and professionalism. The manager is responsible for developing a clinical ladder for her department of eight nurses. In the past she has not had problems implementing new programs, but the staff in this department is relatively new. The nurses are older, they have many years of experience, and they are resistant to change.

Questions for Discussion

1. What leadership style will best accomplish this goal?
2. How might the nurse manager motivate the staff to become positively involved?
3. Use one of the decision-making models to decide how to develop the clinical ladder.
4. How might the manager use brainstorming and brainwriting?

References

Adams, J. (1986). *The care and feeding of ideas*. Reading, Mass.: Addison-Wesley Publishing.

Blai, R. (1986). Eight steps to successful problem solving. *Supervisory Management,* 31(1), 7-9.

Blake, R. and Mouton, J. (1962). The developing revolution in management practices. *Training Directors Journal,* 16(7), 29-52.

Claus, K. and Bailey, J. (1975). *Decision making in nursing*. St. Louis: Mosby-Year Book.

Cyert, R. and March, J. (1963). *A behavioral theory of the firm*. Englewood Cliffs, N.J.: Prentice Hall.

Deitzer, B. and Krigline, A. (1988). When making that decision. *Management Solutions,* 33(11), 3-8.

Dubin, R., Homans, G., Mann, F., and Miller, D. (1965). *Leadership and productivity*. San Francisco: Chandler Publishing.

Epstein, S. and Fenz, N. (1965). Steepness of approach and avoidance gradients in humans as a function of experience: Theory and experiment. *Journal of Experimental Psychology,* 70, 1-12.

Freund, C. (1988). Assessing decision making style with type theory. In Henry, B., Arndt, C., Vincenti, D., and Marriner, A., editors: *Dimensions and issues in nursing administration*. Boston: Blackwell Scientific Publications.

Gardner, J. (1986). The tasks of leadership, part 1: getting things done. *Personnel,* 63(10), 20-27.

Gazzaniga, M. (1975). Review of the split brain. *UCLA Educator,* 9-12.

Glassman, E. (1989). Creative problem solving: new techniques. *Supervisory Management,* 34(3), 14-18.

Hage, J. (1980). *Theories of organizations*. New York: John Wiley and & Sons.

Heller, F. (1973). Leadership, decision making, and contingency theory, *Industrial Relations*, 12(2), 183-100.

Hersey, P. and Blanchard, K., (1988). *Management of organizational behavior* (ed.5). Englewood Cliffs, N.J.: Prentice Hall.

Hoyt, M. and Janis, I. (1975). Increasing adherence to a stressful decision via a motivational balance sheet procedure: A field experiment. *Journal of Personality and Social Psychology*, 31, 833-839.

Janis, I. and Mann, L. (1977). *Decision making*. New York: Free Press.

Mann, L., Janis, I., and Chaplin, R. (1969). The effects of anticipation of forthcoming information on predecisional processes. *Journal of Personality and Social Psychology*, 11, 10-16.

March, J. and Simon, H. (1958). *Organizations*. New York: John Wiley & Sons.

Myers, I. and McCaulley, M. (1985). *A guide to the development and use of the Myers-Briggs Type Indicator*. Palo Alto, Calif.: Consulting Psychologists Press.

Rodrigues, C. (1988). Identifying the right leader for the right situation. *Personnel*, 65(9), 43-46.

Scharf, A. (1985). Secrets of problem solving. *Industrial Management*, 27(5), 7-11.

Segall, L. and Meyers, C. (1988). Taking aim at problems, *Management Solutions*, 33(2), 5-8.

Shapero, A. (1985). Managing creative professionals. *Research Management*, 28(2), 23-28.

Sperry, R. (1975). Left-brain, right-brain. *Saturday Review*. 30-33.

Steiner, G. (1965). *The creative organization*. Chicago: The University of Chicago Press.

Stogdill, R. (1948). Personal factors associated with leadership: a survey of the literature. *Journal of Psychology*, 25, 35-71.

Tjosvold, D., Wedley, W., and Field, R. (1986). Constructive controversy, the Vroom-Yetton model, and managerial decision making. *Journal of Occupational Behaviour*, 7, 125-138.

Vroom, V. and Yetton, P. (1973). *Leadership and decision making*. Pittsburgh: University of Pittsburgh Press.

Wiberg, L., (1988). Should you change your leadership style? *Management Solutions*, 33(1), 5-12.

12

ELLEN LYNCH

Organizational Networking
Empowerment Through Politics

CHAPTER OBJECTIVES

- ☐ Explain the relationship between networking and transformational power.
- ☐ Describe the technique used by a transformational leader to enable others to assimilate and embrace the vision.
- ☐ Contrast and compare the concepts of "traditional" power, empowerment, and politics.
- ☐ Describe the environment that fosters empowerment.
- ☐ Explain how self-empowerment occurs and its relation to the empowerment of others.
- ☐ Describe nursing's golden window of opportunity for developing autonomy and enhancing professional practice.

The Stage Is Set For Change

Revolution! Diversification! Change! Joint venture! Entrepreneurship! Empowerment! These are terms frequently used to describe what is occurring in the
health care delivery system in this country. Health care has been in the midst of
a fundamental transition that has been energized by a shift "from a product
driven focus dominated by professionals to a market-driven focus dominated by
customers, from care taking to risk taking, and from operational to strategic
management" (Shortell, 1989, p. 9). Historically, health care institutions have
considered that the physician who admits patients into the system was the
customer. Most hospitals have been community-benefit organizations with the
primary purpose of caring for persons in varying stages of illness, using
up-to-date technology, high quality equipment, adequate facilities, special
services, and highly qualified support staff. Until the 1980s, hospital administrators focused on internal operational management and had few concerns about
financial viability, because of the "cost-plus" reimbursement system. There was
little risk-taking and limited competition. During the 1960s and 1970s
administrators didn't worry about costs. The primary concern was keeping up
with the latest technology, expanding facilities, and providing highly qualified
staff and an up-to-date environment in which the physician could work
(Starkweather and Carman, 1988).

During the same two decades, health care costs rose dramatically. From
1965 to 1984 the cost of care increased 10 times. In 1965 the average cost for
a hospital day was $41; in 1985 it was $432. In the 1990s the cost has been
projected to reach $800. Run-away health care costs were driven by a third party
cost-based reimbursement system that made in-hospital care the first choice for
treating the sick. This system did not support preventive care, in which people
are helped in taking care of themselves. The prevailing philosophy seemed to
push for more patients, more tests, and longer stays, all providing more revenue
for hospitals and physicians. Patients chose this system and often sought
unnecessary care, since they did not have to worry about costs (Califano, 1986).
Another factor contributing to this upward trend was rapid innovation in
technology. The 1970s saw such advances as coronary bypass grafts, joint
replacement, total parenteral nutrition, and computerized axial tomography
(CAT) scanning. This was followed in the next decade with the development of
magnetic resonance imaging (MRI) and heart and liver transplants. Meanwhile,
hospitals increasingly had to pay more for what they purchased because of
inflation. The high technology called for "high touch" and highly skilled
employees, all of which greatly increased personnel budgets (Inglehart, 1989).

The biggest buyers of health care — the government and corporations — felt
the financial bite of rising health costs and began to look for ways to slow the
escalation. These costs had to be controlled, or society would see health care costs
doubling every 6 to 7 years. At that rate, America would get into a position in

which it could not compete in the world market, and health care would be rationed, with regulations governing who would live and die (Califano, 1986).

The revolution in the health care delivery system was ignited by the passage of the Tax Equity and Fiscal Responsibility Act of 1983, which provided a totally new approach to financial reimbursement for health care. This new system was based on prospective payment for Medicare recipients, which paid a predetermined amount for a specific diagnostic related group (DRG). All Medicare patients were placed into a DRG, and thus the amount of reimbursement for hospitals was determined. Whether the hospital made money depended upon the organization's efficiency, cost effectiveness, and ability to reduce the length of time the patient stayed in the hospital. If the patient stayed past the point where the cost of care exceeded the predetermined payment, the hospital lost money (Califano, 1986). The goals of this system were to "control the growth of federal expenditures under Medicare and to promote increased cost effectiveness" (Sheingold, 1989, p. 192).

As this new system was phased in, fear, anxiety, and panic gripped health care organizations, particularly hospitals. They had to find ways to cut costs, reduce the patient's length of stay, and at the same time remain profitable while continuing to provide quality care. Personnel budgets were cut, employees were laid off or changed to part-time, nonessential programs and services were retrenched or eliminated, and physicians were pressured to adjust their practices to ensure lower costs and shorter stays for their patients. These events created conflict among administrators, employees, physicians, and other professional staff.

As the length of stay dropped and physicians began monitoring admissions and prescribing fewer diagnostic studies and treatments, revenues of the institutions dropped. In many areas a surplus of beds resulted in closing units or reducing the number of beds in service. This downward trend in admissions and length of stay was greater than anticipated, and it is predicted to continue. For example, in 1982 there were 170 admissions per 1000 patient days; by 1987 it had decreased to 138; and by 1995 it is projected to be about 123. The average length of stay has continued to drop and may reach 5.6 days by 1995. With an increasing number of Americans lacking health insurance (31.1 million, or 15% of the population in 1987) hospitals will bear the financial burden of uncompensated care, rising from 4.6% of total revenue in 1987 to about 8.3% in 1995 (Moyer, 1989; Westbury, 1988). It has been predicted that about 700 of the nation's hospitals (10%) will close by 1995 because of the inability to remain financially solvent. Smaller hospitals are the ones most likely to close (Westbury, 1988).

In concert with the federal prospective payment system, corporations and insurance companies have changed their health care reimbursement systems to pass more financial responsibility on to the individual through co-payment and deductibles. The trend is toward health promotion and outpatient and home care. Reimbursement for outpatient services, home care, physical examinations, and health maintenance has reduced hospital admissions and encouraged care in the less expensive arenas. This has given individuals the incentive to monitor their health care expenditures and shop for lower-cost services. Health care that was primarily centered in hospitals began to move into other types of less costly facilities, such as free-standing outpatient surgicenters, convenient care centers, diagnostic facilities in physicians' offices, and wellness and fitness centers. The government encouraged people to organize offices, and wellness and fitness centers. The government encouraged people to organize into units or groups of health service buyers such as Health Maintenance Organizations (HMO) and Preferred Provider Organizations (PPO). Thus, competition among providers dramatically increased (Bopp and Hicks, 1984).

It became obvious that if hospitals continued to depend on inpatient care to create sufficient revenue, then bankruptcy could follow. Consequently, it became necessary for institutions to reconceptualize their purposes in view of the changing environment. The past practice of projecting the future based upon the status quo was no longer a valid method of planning. Health care institutions awoke to the fact that they were businesses that needed to make a profit, were in real competition with others, and had to think and act accordingly (Ives and Kerfort, 1989). They had to answer the question, "What business are we in – inpatient care of the sick or health care with a broader scope of possibilities?" In *Megatrends,* Naisbitt (1984) compared the situation of hospitals to that of the railroads. He pointed out that one of the problems with the railroads is that they "should have known they were in the transportation business and not just railroading" (p. 88). The situation would have been different if they had decided to move from the railroad business to the transportation business. A good success story is seen in the Singer Company, which has been known for its sewing machines and now is becoming an aerospace company (Naisbitt, 1984).

Many health care organizations have responded to the uncertain, unstable, changing system by reorganizing and diversifying. Hospitals are beginning to follow the trends set by other businesses in response to the move from an industrial to an information society. The traditional centralized hierarchy that restricted power to a few is failing. What is emerging is a decentralized network style of organization and management that creates horizontal, vertical, and diagonal linkages among people and groups. This move recognizes that it is the people within the organization who have the potential to make the needed pervasive changes (Naisbitt, 1984).

Departments within the organization are pushed to function like small businesses and take on entrepreneurial roles. This involves finding new solutions to problems and creating new products and services by tapping existing expertise within the department. It requires a leadership that can enable and develop the entrepreneurial skills of employees. Flexibility, creativity, ownership, and authenticity are essential attributes to foster within the new organization. This can be accomplished only by creative transformational leadership that empowers others and creates leaders who lead with their hearts as well as with their minds (Cottingham, 1988). These elements take place within a system of intra- and inter-organizational networking.

Network-Matrix for Change

It is during times of intense change, when individuals and groups have feelings of insecurity, powerlessness, and loss of control, that networks begin to emerge. Networks represent linkages between and among those who recognize mutual threats, problems, needs, and goals that cannot be resolved or satisfied by traditional structures and relationships. Networks are open systems, cooperative and not competitive. As the antidote to alienation, they supply the strategy by which transformation of an organizational or social structure can occur. It is the networking process that is important to discuss. This process is self-generating and self-organizing. It consists of people communicating, sharing ideas and information, and offering support and direction to each other. This leads to the establishment of specific networks that can foster the building of a positive power base. Networks work with other networks and thus have tremendous power for directing change. As the traditional system fails to meet the needs of the people and solve growing problems, employees begin to band together into networks that have the potential to replace the traditional hierarchies (Naisbitt, 1984; Persons and Wieck, 1985; Ferguson, 1987).

Looking at what followed the retrenchment in health care corporations, one can see reorganization beginning to occur, allowing more freedom and flexibility in diversification. Holding companies have been established with subsidiaries that provide a variety of new services, both for-profit and not-for-profit. Such services as home health care, extended care facilities, birthing centers, and diagnostic services—to name only a few—have developed into a new interorganizational network that is a macrosocial unit comprised of numerous interdependent and consequently nonautonomous organizations (Koenig, 1981).

Other types of networks have evolved that link corporations together to yield greater purchasing power at reduced costs, to have access to a wider variety of resources, to share expertise and services, and to establish greater political influence. The organizational arrangements that occur within the network take many forms. One example is seen in coalitions of two independent institutions for joint ventures in programs or services; another is corporate ownership of multiple institutions, such as the for-profit Hospital Corporation of America. The advantages of such multi-institutional systems were thought to be (1) organizational survival and greater political power as transaction networks; (2)

access to information and resources (i.e., money, physical commodities, and clients); and (3) new markets that are acquired and shared (Freund and Mitchel, 1985; Koenig, 1981). As the contingencies and complexities within the network increase, the expanded governance that must occur has been in the direction of an open, decentralized system (Koenig, 1981). The traditional bureaucratic structure cannot provide the horizontal linkages that networks offer (Naisbitt, 1984). Consequently, the old hierarchies are crumbling and a new type of management and leadership is evolving within a network system.

Simultaneous with the move to greater diversity and interorganizational networking there are new linkages occurring within each organization as a result of intraorganizational networking. The people within the organization are striving to claim their rights, have more control over the work environment, and find greater meaning in their work and life. Networking within the organization is tremendously liberating because it is the individual that is the primary value in a network. The network becomes an arena for personal exploration, autonomy, and group action. It is intimate while serving as a base for growth and power (Ferguson, 1987).

The move toward networking is an open window allowing the needed change within the industry to occur, turning impotency and impending failure into success. The greatest strength and resource for creativity, innovation, and problem resolution is in the people at all levels of the organization. As Bennis (1986) points out, "The idea of a relatively small group of movers and shakers who get things done is obsolete" (p. 65). With networks there are more stakeholders who are concerned and verbal about how the business is conducted and controlled. As problems grow, the more power is diffused and the more people have to be involved. In an attempt to find common characteristics of effective leaders, Bennis (1986) studied 80 chief executive officers and 10 innovative leaders. He found that among the competencies two things seemed outstanding. These were the ability to create and communicate a vision to gain support and induce commitment and the ability through empowerment to create an environment that would tap and use the abilities and energy of others. In so doing, the organization could become "a blending of each individual's uniqueness into collective action" (Bennis, 1986, p. 68). Bennis called this process transformative power, in which there is an exchange between the leader and the led with participative response.

Negotiating the Vision Through Agreement and Trust

In the process of crystallizing and communicating a vision in such a way that others will assimilate it and embrace it, the transformative leader must be able to develop coalitions and support. There are always those within the organization who oppose pursuing the vision and feel threatened if the perceived results will not fit in with their vested interests. According to Block (1987), after creating the vision the "task is to walk the tight rope between being strong advocates for our beliefs and not terminally alienating others in the process" (p. 130). This requires political savvy, sensitivity to others, and the ability to negotiate agreement and trust. Agreement or opposition is often centered on the clarity of the vision, and the degree of trust is built upon the presence of justice and integrity. It is important to negotiate the vision with carefully identified advocates and adversaries in a positive political way. As depicted in Figure 12-1, Block (1987) suggested a matrix using the elements of high and low trust and agreement, enabling identification of persons as allies or adversaries.

The allies that appear in the upper right corner of the matrix are those who share the vision and purpose and with whom there is a trusting reciprocal relationship. It is important to recognize that some individuals who are thought to be opponents are really allies who support the vision but are critical in a way that sharpens and improves efforts to reach the goal. Persons who are identified as opponents are those who disagree with the vision but with whom there is a high trusting relationship. These persons also serve an important role in challenging and consequently stimulating more effective strategies and clearer vision. It is important to know the difference between opponents and adversaries. This difference lies in the degree of trusting relationship. There is less trust with adversaries than opponents. Bedfellows are those who are in agreement with the vision but with whom there is a low amount of trust. Because of this, it is important to avoid the inclination to be manipulative, instead striving for an open, honest, clear statement of support for the vision. Setting a trusting example that builds integrity may help transform the bedfellows into stronger and more trustworthy supporters (Block, 1987).

Adversaries are those with whom negotiating agreement and trust has not worked. These persons consume time and energy that should be spent elsewhere. Once the adversaries have been carefully identified as such, the best course of action is to let them go. One should stop trying to persuade or destroy them and, instead, should indicate at least an understanding of their position (Block, 1987).

Another problem the leader faces is with the "fence-sitter": one who refuses to take a position. These persons are cautious, pessimistic, and concerned about failure. They need to be gently urged to take a position; but as with the adversaries, time and energy should not be wasted on trying to change them. The objective of the visionary leader is to move people toward the upper right quadrant of the matrix, to increased trust and agreement. Most of the leader's time should be spent with allies and opponents. The best way to gain this support and trust is through "a well-articulated vision statement and authentic behavior" (Block, 1987, p. 151). In a spirit of openness and participative response,

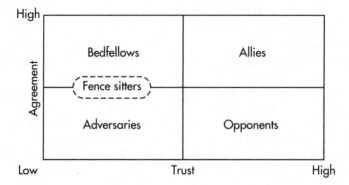

Fig. 12-1. From Block, P.: *The empowered manager: Positive political skills at work.* San Francisco: Jossey-Bass, 1987.

organizational integrity will develop as each individual is provided the opportunity to achieve personal recognition, integrity, and authenticity.

Entrepreneur to Intrapreneur

As defined by Webster (1985, p. 414) the entrepreneur is "one who organizes, manages, and assumes risks of a business." This implies that an entrepreneur would be self-employed, innovative, and independent in a business enterprise. A corporation may be an entrepreneur in identifying, developing, and aggressively marketing new products, services, and programs within a market area, engaging in a competitive relationship with other companies. For such a business to be successful in its entrepreneurial adventures, it must have leaders and employees who have the qualities of an entrepreneur. These are persons who are always eager to expand or change their careers and openly express dissatisfaction with the status quo. They tend to be energetic, risk-takers, and visionary, and they often see opportunities that others miss or do not understand. These corporate entrepreneurs are persons who question, test limits, and push the innovative process for action (Kanter, 1984; Silver, 1987).

In the traditional hierarchical structure, where power is vested in a few, entrepreneurs are seen as "free spirits." They represent a threat, create unrest, question the system, and are labeled troublemakers or power seekers. Unfortunately, this has frequently led to their suppression, discipline, transfer, or termination. The nearsighted, insecure, and inexperienced manager may view these persons as a hindrance to the smooth operation of the department. Eliminating them would help maintain the status quo, but it could also help destroy the organization.

In the dawn of the new economy and organizational networking, many businesses have begun to recognize these entrepreneurs as an asset and have initiated the idea of intrapreneurship as a way to grow by attracting and keeping the most creative and innovative people. The intrapreneur is one who organizes, manages, and has fiscal and legal responsibility for a product line or service while maintaining an affiliation with the parent institution. The corporation that fosters such an organization becomes a federation or network of entrepreneurs. Examples of the products of such intrapreneurs can be found in companies such as 3M (Post-its™), IBM (IBM PC), Texas Instruments (Speak and Spell), and Ford (Mustang) (Boyar and Martinson, 1990).

The real challenge is to develop transformational leaders who can find and capitalize upon the contributions of those who possess these abilities. In so doing, the leader facilitates intrapreneurial activities within the organization. These innovators work across boundaries and reach beyond the requirements and limits of their own jobs, not only in scope but also in resources needed to carry out their projects. According to Boyar and Martinson (1990), one of the factors that differentiates intrapreneurs from entrepreneurs is the presence of a team spirit. The intrapreneur works well within the team; entrepreneurs work well within a network system. To initiate and implement change, it is essential for leaders to have the power to move or influence the system to open channels so that people and resources can be mobilized to get things done (Kanter, 1984). This power is basic to innovative results for the organization and is given to managers, intrapreneurs, and entrepreneurs through decentralization.

Philosophy for Empowerment

To move from a bureaucracy to a decentralized network supporting the intrapreneurial spirit and growth, an organization must develop a philosophy and ethic that empowers managers and fosters transformational leadership. In developing such a philosophy it is essential to understand the nature of leadership and its relationship to power and politics.

We are constantly confronted with the existence of power in our businesses, in society, and in world affairs. The usual concerns regard who has the power, how it is distributed, and how it is used or abused. Power, as broadly defined, means the ability to change or influence the behavior and decisions of others (Leininger, 1979). Beeman and Sharkey (1987) described power as "the ability to alter the realities of a situation" and "to change the cause and effect relationship within a situation" (p. 27). Influence is that part of power that reflects the ability to change another's perception of the cause and effect relationship in a situation. The basis of such power can come from many sources: a legitimate position of authority within the organization, possession of information and knowledge, proven expertise, inducement by reward or punishment, and/or the development of respect and charisma (Beeman and Sharkey, 1987). It is necessary to consider power and politics together: one cannot be present or in use without the other. Politics concerns the way an individual or group uses or exchanges power to promote or protect vested interests, concerns, or goals (Leininger, 1979).

The traditional concept of power often places it in a negative frame of reference, as being potentially evil and abusive and as connoting dominance and submission, control and acquiescence, and manipulation through coercion (McFarland, Leonard, and Morris, 1984). Power has been viewed as fixed, so that acquisition of more power by one person means the loss of power by another. An example would be the transfer of political power from one party to the other following an election. This type of power has been common in the institutions of government, church, school, and business. The maneuvering and exchange of such power is political behavior, which is one of the common forms of human behavior. It is learned at an early age through instruction by parents and teachers. Children learn to play games and influence the behavior of others. These political methods used to reach goals and gain resources or advantages were often manipulative and divisive, reflecting the negative side of political power. The goal in today's world should be the use of power with a more positive focus.

In *The Aquarian Conspiracy,* Ferguson (1987) explained politics as the use of power within the context of an organization. When there is conflict, unfair practice, and abuse of power and freedom, a social revolution occurs. Power begins to change hands through an emerging network. A new political paradigm appears as new values are assimilated by the dominant society and passed on to new generations. We can see such a new political paradigm emerging as evidenced by the fall of the Berlin Wall, the rebellion against Apartheid, and the student demonstrations in Tian'anmen Square. It can also be seen in the evolutionary changes in the structure and function of business reflected in decentralization and the development of an intrapreneurial philosophy of management.

As Block (1987) pointed out in *The Empowered Manager,* a revolution has been occurring in many organizations in which the traditional structure, control, and power were fading and attention was turning to the needs of employees to take responsibility for the success of the business. The rate of development of greater insights into human needs and capacities has been more rapid than necessary social changes could occur, forcing a complete transformation of the political system. To restructure society using the traditional methods would prove futile. The change must come through personal revolution. Since individuals make up the institutions, it follows that as the individuals change so will the social structure. Ferguson (1987) defined autarchy as "government by the self" (p. 192). She referred to Confucian writings to describe that once individuals look within and can "verbalize intelligence of the heart" they find order within the self, then within their households, and finally in the state and empire. As such a personal transformation takes place a new perception of power emerges. This process results in self-empowerment. The discovery of a freedom in which one is "free for something, not just from something" (p. 192). This transformation within the person brings with it concern for others and a broader perspective admitting of many realities or contingencies rather than only a single, focused point of view. This lays greater importance on power over one's life as well as respect for the same right in others (Ferguson, 1987). Too often, feelings of helplessness and lack of opportunity are the result of restricted awareness. One must realize that power is not only a function of one's position but, more importantly, a state of mind.

In *The Search for Authenticity,* Bugental (1965) examined the existential view of the human experience in an attempt to release and facilitate the human potential. This, of course, is what the leader strives to achieve with self as well as with co-workers. Individuals strive to be aware of and understand themselves, their world, and how to live in the situations in which they find themselves. They are concerned with being authentic. "A person is authentic in that degree to which his being in the world is unqualified in accord with the givenness of his own nature and the world" (p. 31). To gain a sense of authenticity a person must have an awareness of a given situation and all the contingencies that can affect it. This is an awareness of those contingencies that have shaped, influenced, and caused the current state and also those contingencies that can change the circumstance. A state of uncertainty results in an individual experiencing anxiety. Freedom, which is highly cherished, is surrounded by contingencies. It is affected by many things: the rights of others, accountability for our actions, and potential effects of others' actions. There is no freedom when we know all the determinants, because there is little choice to be made. Freedom comes with having a choice and knowing that it may be an important determinant in the outcome (Bugental, 1965). This choice is our responsibility, and empowerment of self and others comes with being able to act to effect change and direction. We live with contingencies. We are subject to events or influences that we cannot anticipate. However, we can develop an awareness of this and know that we have the potential and responsibility to make a decision and act. We must have the autonomy to make choices and the responsibility to take action that effects alternatives. At the same time we must realize that tragedy or failure is always a possibility and that our awareness and actions cannot change that fact. This is the reality of life (Bugental 1965).

Author-psychiatrist Dr. Viktor Frankl presented his version of existential analysis in *Man's Search for Meaning* (1984). He developed and described logotherapy, a meaning-centered psychotherapy. While he was a prisoner in a German concentration camp during World War II he observed the behavior of fellow prisoners. He discovered that there was one thing over which people had control even when everything else had been taken from them. This was the freedom to choose one's attitude toward a situation and to choose how one would react. The right to control one's attitude and response is a freedom no one can take away. Frankl (1984) emphasized that a person cannot always control what happens, but one can always control one's reactions. It is through this freedom and power to choose that people feel they have control over their environment and destiny and can find meaning in their lives. People have the potential to be self-determining. What they actually become depends on the decisions they make and act upon, not on the conditions around them.

Frankl (1984) proposed that the search for meaning is the primary motivation in a person's life. It is essential for him or her to actualize the meaning in his or her life, and it is to be accomplished outside the self and in the world. The more a person is able to forget himself or herself, commit to a cause, a vision, or another person, the more actualized he or she becomes. One cannot attain self-actualization except as a side effect of self-transcendence.

Managers or leaders who have this understanding and insight into human nature, behavior, and needs, including the need to search for meaning and authenticity, can use it in empowering themselves and others. This knowledge fosters the development of the new leadership mentality that facilitates the creativity, commitment, and self-actualization needed for a dynamic, successful organization.

Throughout this chapter we have referred to leadership, especially transformational leadership. Some would view leadership, which is a special form of power, as a leader making followers do what he or she wants, regardless of the followers' interests. On the contrary, Burns (1978) defined leadership as people who motivate or inspire followers to identify and work toward goals that represent mutual values, needs, and expectations of both the leaders and followers. It is the transformational leader who can achieve this level of leadership that recognizes and builds on followers' need and search for meaning.

The development of this new leader can take place only in an organizational environment having a management philosophy and ethic that centers attention on the ethical and emotional needs of employees. The crisis that is occurring in business, especially health care, is not just fiscal or cultural, but it is also personal, spiritual, and ethical. The leadership must view business and ethics as allies. The effective executive is one who is not only concerned about making a profit but who strives to do so while also recognizing and meeting moral and ethical obligations to clients, employees, and society. Within this authentic environment, all are elevated to a higher level of performance that reflects loyalty, respect, commitment, and self-fulfillment (Koestenbaum, 1987). It is within this environment that the transformational leader can move into a mutual relationship with followers and serve as a role model for the emergence of new leaders.

The difference between the leader and the led is not so much in function but in who initiates the relationship. The leader initiates the exchange and maintains the relationship. The transformational leader shares power and, in so doing, becomes a more powerful leader. The cornerstone of the relationship is made up of a strong moral ethic with mutual respect and purpose from which the intrapreneur can emerge. Block (1987) identifies four elements that are necessary for this type of organization.

1. The belief that authority comes from within. The employees are the ones who know what actions would be best for business.
2. The encouragement of self-expression by providing a setting in which there is trust and in which people can put energy, passion, and enthusiasm into their work.
3. The expectation of a commitment, as opposed to sacrifice. This serves as a way to find meaning and self-expression.
4. The creation of an organization based on the first three beliefs, clearly reflecting in all interactions that self-expression, commitment, and ownership are good for business.

Health care in this country is in a jet stream of change—the same kind of change that is occurring in social and political structures throughout the world. It is driven by political, economic, and personal forces that are slowly toppling the rigid walls of the traditional hierarchy, opening new vistas for organizational restructuring and creating a different paradigm for management. The old hierarchy, in which power was centered in a few, is giving way to an organizational network with shared power. The network structure forms a base to link leaders with followers in such a way that each becomes an important player in identifying and striving toward a common purpose. This new paradigm is cultured through the medium of transformed leadership, in which the leader, through the use of positive political strategy, is able to place the followers at the heart of the endeavor and to create an openness that can release and use creative ideas and can find meaning in life. Empowerment occurs as all within the network share the same vision, pool their energy and creativity, and move toward the same goal in a way that is effective and meaningful. Effective leadership and organizational success should be measured by the extent to which the shared vision, goals, and power create within each person a compelling drive to excel while at the same time find meaning in work and life.

☐ Implications for Nursing

Nursing has long struggled to enhance its autonomy, political influence, knowledge base, and professional image to gain fuller recognition as a profession. Because nurses have been bound by the hierarchical, centralized structure of health care systems, it has been difficult to make much progress toward those ends. However, within the past decade nursing has found itself in the midst of tremendous forces of change occurring in the health care system. Health care agencies are following the direction of other successful businesses and moving from a highly structured, autonomous business environment to a more diversified, decentralized network that is market driven.

With the competitive challenge of controlling and reducing costs while increasing quality and productivity, there is a need to foster both entrepreneurial and intrapreneurial creativity. This softening of the hierarchical structure within the organization has presented an open window of opportunity for nursing to make major strides toward achieving professional autonomy.

According to Peter Block (1987), when the traditional structure begins to fade there is a need for individuals (employees) to take responsibility for the success of the organization. As this happens in health care, networks begin to form and power begins to change hands as a new political paradigm begins to emerge. New values are developed and assimilated. The nurse executives and leaders who recognize and understand the dynamics of these evolving networks can direct energies and political powers in very positive and constructive ways, moving toward a system of shared governance.

With the increasing complexity and expansion of health care and services, there have developed high turnover rates and shortages of qualified professional nurses. It has become essential for nurse executives to find ways of attracting, recruiting, developing, and retaining qualified professional staff. This necessitates knowing and acknowledging what these professionals expect and value in their professional and personal lives. In many situations it demands reorganization and changes in the philosophy of management.

Nursing must develop interorganizational and intraorganizational networks and coalitions that expand its information, resources, and power base to successfully develop nursing governance within the health care organization. This involves developing transformational leaders who are self-empowered and can empower others to discover and use their unique skills and creativity to their fullest. This would stimulate entrepreneurial and intrapreneurial development that would not only enhance the institution's competitive position but would also place quantitative and qualitative values on nursing practice. As this type of practice setting emerges, nurses can experience a sense of ownership, commitment, and meaning in their professional practice.

Through strong networking and sharing wisdom, experience, expertise, and resources, a greater sense of collegiality and camaraderie develops, and nursing can be well on its way to becoming one of the most powerful and politically effective professional disciplines in the health care arena. The time has come for nurse executives and leaders to focus more intensely on the development of authentic transformational leaders who share power and whose leadership reflects Block's (1987) four elements in the organizational environment (see p. 14).

◻ *Application to Nursing: Case Study*

A 600-bed tertiary care, not-for-profit teaching hospital is located in an urban area where there are three other full-service hospitals of similar size and service. Within the community is a university with a school of nursing having associate, baccalaureate, and masters degree programs. The hospitals are highly competitive in terms of services, programs, and staff.

To meet the demands of the rapidly changing health care market, the hospital has reorganized as one of several subsidiaries under a holding company. The hospital remains a not-for-profit institution. This reorganization included for-profit subsidiaries, a number of which provide special services to a network of smaller community hospitals within the region. The hospital administrative team has assigned the department directors the task of encouraging entrepreneurial and intrapreneurial activities to provide marketable programs and services. Within the past two years the hospital has become a member of a national organizational network of not-for-profit hospitals. This move was made to place the hospital in a better position to compete with other hospital chains. Membership provided better access to capital, volume purchasing at lower costs, shared resources, consultation, and management development. In some of the other member hospitals the nursing departments have been moving toward reorganization and shared governance.

The vice president for nursing has been in the position for 3 years and has been successful in moving the nursing department from a centralized to a more decentralized organization with the introduction of a participative management philosophy. Her vision for the future is to implement a shared governance system that fosters creativity and growth of the professional staff. This concept has the support of hospital administration. Over half of the nursing directors have master's degrees and the others are encouraged to work toward the degree. The nursing staff has been relatively stable in the past, recruiting from the nursing programs in the area.

The nursing department, however, is experiencing an acute shortage of registered nurses and an escalating turnover rate. Outside agencies have been used increasingly for supplemental staffing. This has created even more staff concern because of the lack of orientation and lower quality of these nurses. There is much anxiety and discontent over increased workload, overtime, fear of legal risk, and decreased quality of care. There have been numerous requests from staff for more flexibility in hours and more choice in regard to 8-, 10-, and 12-hour shifts. The nurses frequently complain that management does not listen and does not understand their problems. Even though nurses participate on committees, their input is not often reflected in the decision making. On two of the units, some of the nurses have asked the director to consider the use of self-scheduling and job sharing.

At a nursing executive meeting, the directors discussed the growing problems, rising discontent, and frustration. The directors immediately acknowledged the capability, loyalty, and qualifications of the nursing staff, but they believed morale was rapidly deteriorating. The vice president explored with the directors the possible factors contributing to the problems and suggested developing plans to move toward a system of shared governance. She believed this would establish a more positive environment for creative growth. The directors expressed some anxiety about moving toward such a change, admitting that they did not have enough knowledge of the concept or how to direct the change without losing control.

Questions for Discussion

1. What might be the window of opportunity for this nursing department in moving toward shared governance?
2. Discuss the wisdom of the vice president for nursing in recommending that moving toward shared governance at this time could resolve the problems of the department.
3. Identify the interorganizational and intraorganizational networks that need to be developed or strengthened.
4. What immediate actions could the management team take to respond to the nursing staff's requests and complaints and at the same time provide an introduction to the concept of shared governance?
5. How might the vice president for nursing identify the degree of trust and agreement with regard to the organizational direction of the department?
6. How might the management team capitalize on the hospital's membership in the coalition of not-for-profit hospitals in resolving problems and moving the department toward reorganization?

References

Beeman, D.R. and Sharkey, T.W. (1987). The use and abuse of corporate politics. *Business Horizons,* (Indiana University Graduate School of Business), *30*(2), 26-30.

Bennis, W. (1986). Transformative power and leadership. In Sergiovanni, T.J., and Corbally, J.E., editors: *Leadership and organizational culture* (pp. 64-71). Chicago: University of Illinois Press.

Block, P. (1987). *The empowered manager: Positive political skills at work.* San Francisco: Jossey-Bass.

Bopp, K. and Hicks, L. (1984). Strategic management in health care. *Nursing Economics,* 2(2), 93-101.

Boyar, D.C. and Martinson, D.J. (1990). Intrapreneurial group practice. *Nursing and Health Care, 11*(1), 29-32.

Bugental, Jr. F.T. (1965). *The search for authenticity.* (p. 14, 15). New York: Holt, Rinehart and Winston.

Burns, J.M. (1978). *Leadership.* New York: Harper & Row.

Califano, Jr. J. (1986). *American health care revolution: who lives? who dies? who pays?* New York: Random House.

Cottingham, C. (1988). Transformational leadership: a strategy for nursing. *Today's O.R. Nurse, 10*(6), 24-27.

Ferguson, M. (1987). *The aquarian conspiracy.* Los Angeles: J.P. Tarcher.

Frankl, V. (1984). *Man's search for meaning* (ed. 2). New York: Simon and Schuster.

Freund, C.M. and Mitchel, J. (1985). Multi-institutional systems: the new arrangements. *Nursing Economics, 3*(1), 24-29.

Inglehart, J.K. (1989). From research to rationing: a conversation with William B. Schwartz. *Health Affairs, 8*(3), 60-75.

Ives, J. and Kerfort, K. (1989). Pitfalls and promises of diversification. *Nursing Economics, 7*(4), 200-203.

Kanter, R.M. (1984). *The change masters.* New York: Simon and Schuster.

Koenig, Jr. R. (1981). The interorganizational network as a system: toward a conceptual framework. In England, G.W., Negandi, A.R., and Wilpert, B., editors: The functioning of complex organizations (pp. 275-302). Cambridge, Mass.: Oelge-schlager, Guern. & Hain.

Koestenbaum, P. (1987). *The heart of business.* New York: Saybrook Publishing.

Leininger, M. (1979). Territoriality, power, and creative leadership in administrative nursing contexts. In McFarland, D.E., and Shiflett, N., editors: *Powers in Nursing.* Nursing Dimensions, 7(2), Summer, 1979, 33-42. (Reprinted from *Power: use it or lose it.* New York: National League for Nursing, 1977).

McFarland, G., Leonard, S., and Morris, M. (1984). Power: nature, acquisition, and strategies. *Nursing leadership and management: contemporary strategies* (pp. 202-222). New York: John Wiley & Sons.

Moyer, M.E. (1989). A revised look at the number of uninsured Americans. *Health Affairs, 8*(2), 102-110.

Naisbitt, J. (1984). *Megatrends.* New York: Warner Books.

Persons, C.B. and Wieck, L. (1985). Networking: a power strategy. *Nursing Economics,* 3(1), 53-57.

Sheingold, S.H. (1989). The first 3 years of PPS: impact on medicare costs. *Health Affairs,* 191-204.

Shortell, S. (1989). New directions in hospital governance. *Hospital and Health Services Administration,* 34(1), 7-23.

Silver, A.D. (1987). The entrepreneurial revolution in health care delivery. *Health Care Strategic Management,* 5(6), 15-18.

Starkweather, D. and Carman, J. (1988). The limits of power in hospital markets. *Medical Care Review,* 45(1), 5-48.

Webster's Ninth New Collegiate Dictionary (1985). Springfield, Mass.: Merriam-Webster.

Westbury, Jr. S.A. (1988). The future of health care: changes and choices. *Nursing Economics,* 6(2), 59-62.

Index